Cambridge Regional Geogra[phy]

Editors Harry Tolley, *School of Education, Uni[...]*
Keit[h] [O]rrell, *Department of Education, [...]*

The South West

Adrian Lunnon
School of Education, University of Exeter

Bryan Stephenson
School of Education, University of Exeter

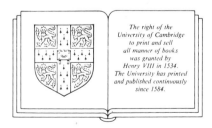

*The right of the
University of Cambridge
to print and sell
all manner of books
was granted by
Henry VIII in 1534.
The University has printed
and published continuously
since 1584.*

Cambridge University Press

Cambridge
New York   Port Chester
Melbourne   Sydney

Published by the Press Syndicate of the University of Cambridge
The Pitt Building, Trumpington Street, Cambridge CB2 1RP
32 East 57th Street, New York, NY 10022, USA
10 Stamford Road, Oakleigh, Melbourne 3166, Australia

First published 1990

Printed in Great Britain by
The University Press, Cambridge

British Library cataloguing in publication data

Lunnon, Adrian
  The South West. – (Cambridge regional geography).
  1. England. South-west England. Human geographical
features
  I. Title II. Stephenson, Bryan
  304.2'09423

ISBN 0 521 27500 8

Acknowledgements

The publishers would like to thank the following for permission to reproduce
material:

ARC (fig 4.12); Agfa Gevaert (fig 6.1); Automobile Association (fig 7.7(c));
Avon Rubber (fig 6.1); R.S. Barron, *The Geology of Wiltshire*, Moonraker Press
(fig 3.19); BP (fig 4.13); Bournemouth Department of Tourism (fig 7.9(c)); Bristol
Economic Development Office (fig 6.17); British Aerospace (fig 6.7); British Rail
(fig 6.7); British Telecom (fig 8.11); Brooklands Aircraft Co. (fig 6.8); Cadbury
(fig 6.1); Central Electricity Generating Board (fig 8.17); Clarks (figs 6.1, 6.4);
CoSIRA (fig 6.12(a)); CPRE (fig 5.11); Dartmoor National Park (fig 7.13); Dalgety
(fig 6.1); Devon County Council (figs 8.7, 9.4); Gwen Ellis, *All my moonshine*,
Venton Educational Ltd (fig 7.15); English China Clays (fig 4.9); English Estates
(fig 6.12(a)); English Tourist Board (figs 7.5, 7.6); Exmouth Journal Ltd (fig 8.9);
Forest of Dean Heritage Centre (fig 7.17(a)); Ginsters (fig 6.3); R.R. Gould and
R.R. White, *The Mental Maps of British School Leavers* (fig 1.3); *The Guardian*
(figs 4.3, 4.20(a)); ICI (figs 6.1, 6.6); Jaeger (fig 6.1); Kiddicraft (fig 6.1); Lalonde
Bros and Parham (fig 6.16); Lukes (fig 6.3); Millers (fig 6.3); Penwith District
Council (fig 7.17(b)); Plessey (fig 6.1); Plymouth City Council (fig 9.15);
The Post Office (fig 9.5); N. Punnett, *People in the Physical Landscape*, Macdonald
Education (fig 3.27); Racal (fig 6.1); Rolls Royce (fig 6.1); South West Water
(figs 4.15, 4.16, 4.17, 4.18); Thamesdown Borough Council (figs 6.10, 9.14);
Trethorne Leisure Farm (fig 9.12); Unigate Dairies (figs 6.1, 6.2); The Usher
Society (fig 4.2); Van Heusen (fig 6.1); West Air Photography (figs 2.12(b), 3.11,
3.29, 8.5); *Western Morning News* (figs 4.20(c), 6.9, 6.14, 10.4); *The Western Times*
(figs 2.3, 2.4, 2.13, 6.11, 9.2, 10.1); Westland (fig 6.7); Christine Whittle
(fig 7.16(b)); Wiggins Teape (fig 6.1); Wiltshire County Council (figs 7.16(a), 7.19).

Cover design by Pavel Büchler.

WV

Contents

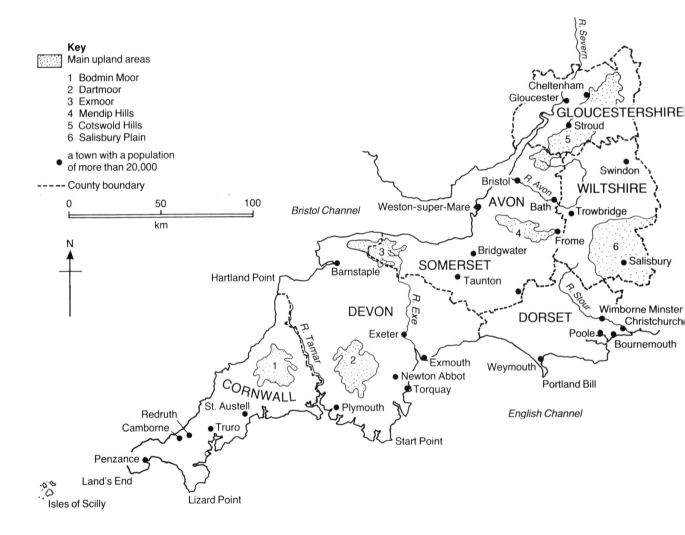

Key

Main upland areas

1 Bodmin Moor
2 Dartmoor
3 Exmoor
4 Mendip Hills
5 Cotswold Hills
6 Salisbury Plain

● a town with a population of more than 20,000

- - - - County boundary

```
0          50         100
|          |           |
        km
```

N

R. Severn

Cheltenham

Gloucester

GLOUCESTERSHIRE

Stroud

5

Swindon

Bristol

R. Avon

WILTSHIRE

Bristol Channel

Weston-super-Mare

AVON

Bath

Trowbridge

4

Frome

6

Salisbury

Bridgwater

SOMERSET

Taunton

R. Exe

Wimborne Minster

DORSET

Christchurch

R. Stour

Hartland Point

Barnstaple

3

DEVON

Exeter

Poole

Bournemouth

R. Tamar

Exmouth

Weymouth

2

Newton Abbot

Torquay

Portland Bill

1

English Channel

CORNWALL

Plymouth

Redruth

St. Austell

Camborne

Truro

Start Point

Penzance

Land's End

Isles of Scilly

Lizard Point

4

Images of the South West

Views and thoughts

1. Thorns and gorse, sea and sand,
   These are things in Devon land.
   Ducks and boats, fish and nets,
   These are things in River Exe.

2. Sir Walter Raleigh born and raised,
   In this land, so clean and praised.
   Sir Francis Drake, Plymouth
     knows,
   That when he lived he played
     bowls.

3. The villages, the quaint old
     church,
   Upon the belfry bats did perch;
   Sleep by day, wake at night,
   Bound to give someone a fright.

4. Plymouth, Exmouth,
     Teignmouth too,
   Where men are fishing in waters
     blue;
   They get a bite and have to fight,
   For their livelihood is true.

Devonshire by Reece Precious (aged 16)

Fig. 1.1. Thoughts which a family living in Birmingham have about South West England.

Standard Regions
The UK is divided into these to help the economic planning of the nation. Therefore they are also known as Economic Planning Regions.

perception
The way you see or feel about a place.

These words are how one teenager views a part of South West England. Fig. 1.1 shows the thoughts which a family living in Birmingham have about the same part of the United Kingdom.

Ask members of your teaching group to write down the first three things which come into their minds when you say 'South West England'. Look at their lists. Count up how many times each thought has been listed. What are the top five?

The South West is one of eleven **Standard Regions** of the UK. As you can see opposite, it contains the counties of Avon, Cornwall (including the Isles of Scilly), Devon, Dorset, Gloucestershire, Somerset and Wiltshire. The region covers nearly 2.5 million hectares, which makes it England's largest Standard Region. It stretches 350 kilometres from east to west. Being so large, it contains many geographical contrasts. For example, isolated west Cornwall contrasts with the bustling areas beside the M4 motorway to the north; east Wiltshire, with its small amount of manufacturing industry, is in complete contrast to busy Avon with its high-tech activities.

Think of one place you have visited, perhaps on holiday. What do you remember about it?

Perhaps your memories are about the people you met, or about the weather, or about the things which you were able or not able to do while you were there. The whole bundle of thoughts and feelings makes up your **perception** of that place.

In the same way, you build up a perception of your home area. Because it is where you live, you probably have a good deal of personal knowledge and feeling about it. Your friends can also

5

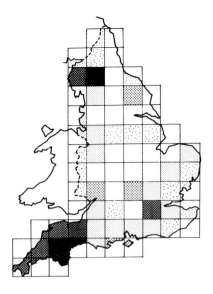

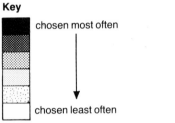

chosen most often

chosen least often

Fig. 1.2. Where 200 adults would most like to live in England.

know it well and have certain feelings about it. However, their bundles of knowledge and feeling may be quite different from yours. If so, they would have different perceptions of the very same home area.

As a result of living in or visiting places, you gain first-hand experience of them. This makes up a powerful part of your total perception. There are also many sources which give you second-hand knowledge and feelings of places – books, television, radio, etc. Unlike your first-hand experiences, these feelings and information have been selected by other people before they come to you. There are, therefore, many ways in which you build up your thoughts and feelings about a place, and each one of us forms our own individual perception of an area.

Preferences

Two hundred adults were asked: 'Where in England would you most like to live, if you had complete freedom of choice in your selection?'. Fig. 1.2 maps their preferences. You will see that Cornwall, Devon and parts of Somerset were strongly favoured. The adults who were interviewed actually lived within the South West, and this may have influenced the result. However, when a thousand fifteen-year-olds throughout Great Britain were asked a similar sort of question, a similar pattern of response emerged (fig. 1.3). Their **surface of preference** has a gradient which, in general, slopes downwards from the south to the north of Britain. Locations selected most frequently lie within a broad band which stretches from Land's End to the Strait of Dover.

preference surface
Like a contour map, but instead of showing changes in height above sea-level, it shows the highs and lows (or different strengths) of the preferences.

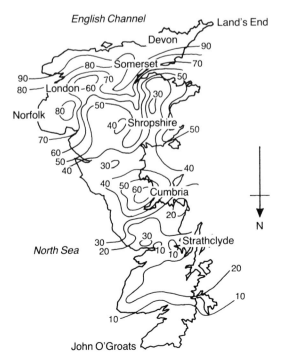

Fig. 1.3. Teenagers' choices.

This is an unusual way of showing Great Britain. Are there any advantages in drawing it 'upside down' in order to display this particular data?

When asked *why* they preferred these locations, both the adults and the teenagers, and those who lived in the chosen areas and those who didn't, all replied that it had something to do with the areas being 'pleasant places' in which to live.

A few years ago, an official Report stated that the three most distinctive features of South West England were:
(a) large areas of natural scenery and beauty;
(b) a pleasant climate;
(c) a comparatively sparse population.

Did any features similar to these come into the top five in the results of the survey of your teaching group?

Fact or fiction?

Are these thoughts and statements based upon facts or upon an individual's imagination? Let us look first of all at the climatic features. Table 1 lists some statistics for towns in England.

Table 1 *Selected climatic data (averages over 35 years) for eight English towns.*

	Average temp in January (°C)	Average temp in July (°C)	Total annual rainfall (mm)	Total annual sunshine (hours)
Located in South West				
Bristol	4.7	16.5	920	1529
Exeter	4.9	16.8	810	1620
Penzance	7.2	16.4	1059	1672
Bournemouth	4.3	16.6	802	1746
Located outside the South West				
Birmingham	3.6	16.7	754	1302
Leeds	3.7	16.6	552	1217
London	3.9	17.8	582	1470
Manchester	3.6	15.7	851	1250

Using this information, write down in each of four columns, the names of the three towns with:
(a) the highest average temperature in January;
(b) the highest average temperature in July;
(c) the lowest total annual rainfall;
(d) the highest total hours of annual sunshine.
Study your lists. Within each column, are the three towns
 (i) all located in the South West?
 (ii) all located outside of the South West?
(iii) divided between a SW and a non-SW location?
Do your findings agree with the general perception that the South West has a climate which is more 'pleasant' than that of other parts of England? What other climatic data would you want to consider before giving a final answer to this question?

For many people, an image of the South West is that it has a mild winter.

Does the evidence in Table 1 support this view?

Snowfall has not been included in the Table, as it is rare compared to other parts of Britain. It falls on an average of only 1.2 days at Penzance, and only on 2.9 days on the higher parts of Dartmoor. When it does occur, the snow doesn't usually lie for long.

The *range of temperature* in the South West is comparatively small (e.g. a range of 8°C in the Isles of Scilly and 11°C at Weymouth). This means that there is an **equable climate**. Factors influencing this include:

(a) the peninsular shape of the South West;
(b) a large part of it lying south of latitude 51°N;
(c) no part of it being more than 50 km from the sea.

Mild winters and springs give the market gardeners of west Cornwall and the Isles of Scilly a big advantage, by helping them to produce flowers, fruit and vegetables earlier than market gardeners in other parts of the United Kingdom.

Do the following photographs illustrate any of the thoughts which the members of your teaching group had of the South West?

range of temperature
The difference between the lowest and highest average monthly temperatures.

equable climate
One which has no extremes of temperature.

Fig. 1.4. East Devon, near Salcombe Regis.

Fig. 1.5. North Cornwall, near St Agnes.

environment
All the natural and human features which surround people and affect their lives.

evaluation
When we give a value (e.g. 'good', 'bad' or 'ugly') to an environment as we perceive it. Another method is to give it a 'score', e.g. between +3 for very attractive and −3 for very unattractive (see also fig. 4.11).

Fig. 1.4 shows a landscape of gentle slopes; the fields are of different shapes and sizes; some are ploughed, other are grazed by sheep or cattle; there are hedgerows, clusters of trees and small groups of buildings. Taken together, these features form an **environment** which many people regard as being attractive or of high quality. You may or may not agree, for like the perception of a place, how we **evaluate** an environment varies from person to person.

What is your evaluation of the landscape shown in fig. 1.5? Do you find it attractive or unattractive? What features have helped you to form this opinion?

The South West has many areas similar to the one shown in fig. 1.5. In fact, Cornwall has over 5,000 hectares of land which is known as derelict land. This is more than any other county in England. It is the result of the mining and quarrying activities carried out in that county in past years.

Another perception of the South West is that it lacks large cities. Is this fact or fiction?

Only one quarter of the South West's population live in large towns (of 100,000 and over). This contrasts with the rest of England and Wales, where the fraction is one half. Bristol is the region's largest settlement, with a population of about 500,000. Plymouth has about 250,000 people. Bournemouth and Swindon, each with about 150,000, come next in order of decreasing population size. Most people in the South West live in small towns or large villages – about one third of them in settlements of fewer than 2,000 people.

Fig. 1.6. (a) Average weekly wages of adults in full-time work, April 1987; (b) regional distribution of unemployment compared to the average for the UK in July 1987; (c) percentage of households living in each region owning cars in 1987.

Economic well-being

How about the South West's economic position? From the selection of data shown below, you can see that average weekly wages are among the lowest in the United Kingdom, and that the

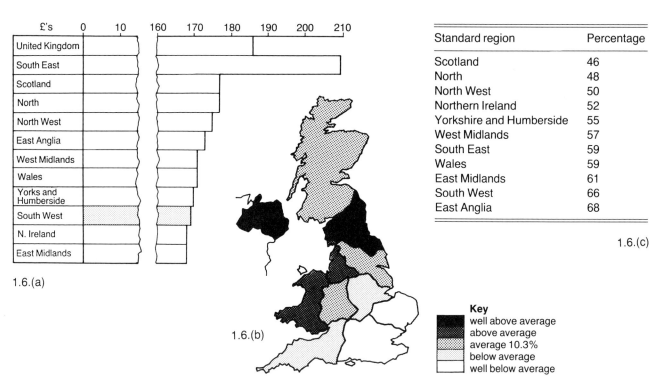

Standard region	Percentage
Scotland	46
North	48
North West	50
Northern Ireland	52
Yorkshire and Humberside	55
West Midlands	57
South East	59
Wales	59
East Midlands	61
South West	66
East Anglia	68

1.6.(c)

1.6.(a)

1.6.(b)

Key
well above average
above average
average 10.3%
below average
well below average

Assisted Areas
These are of two types: **Development Areas**, which receive much money and other help from the Government; **Intermediate Areas** which receive less assistance.

level of unemployment is just a little better than the national average. However, this average figure masks the high unemployment which existed in Redruth (19%) and Falmouth (17%) at that time. For these and other reasons, the South West has for a long time been an **Assisted Area**. It has received much help from national government to improve the environment, the

9

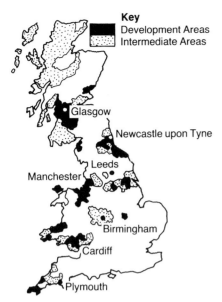

Fig. 1.7. The Assisted Areas of Britain since November 1984.

Core areas

Those areas where facilities, money and people are concentrated. The poorer areas are on the outside, or periphery, of the cores.

Fig. 1.8. Potential for economic growth in the European Community (the numbers are based upon the size of a population and how much money it has to spend). This is another 'surface' map. This time, the lines join places having the same possibilities for economic growth. It shows a core/periphery pattern.

Table 2 *Average house prices in the United Kingdom (March 1988).*

Standard region	Average price of semi-detached house £
South East	73,041
East Anglia	54,989
South West	54,133
West Midlands	36,933
Scotland	36,308
East Midlands	34,656
North West	32,792
Wales	31,431
North	31,059
Yorkshire and Humberside	26,620
Northern Ireland	27,440

living conditions and working opportunities within the region. Improvements have occurred over the years, but as fig. 1.7 shows, certain parts of Cornwall and Devon still require special help. When it is placed in the wider area of the European Community (fig. 1.8), South West England is clearly an area of comparatively low economic standing. So it also receives extra help from a European Regional Development Fund. This map also highlights one of the problems facing the South West – its peripheral location and remoteness from the centres, or **cores**, of economic prosperity. The long narrow shape of the region makes transport linkage difficult and costly (Chapter 8).

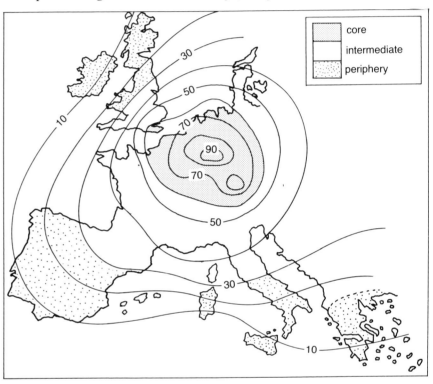

On the other hand, in contrast to other parts of the UK, the level of car ownership in the South West is high (fig. 1.6(c)). Similarly, the possession of domestic capital goods, such as personal computers, video recorders, freezers and dishwashers, is at a high level compared to other regions. However, the cost of buying a house in the South West is the third highest in the United Kingdom (Table 2). So on the one hand, the facts indicate that the South West possesses certain features which are attractive. On the other hand, it has some aspects which are not nearly so good.

Look again at fig. 1.3.
(a) Besides South West England, which other parts of Great Britain have received scores of over 50? Write down why you think they might have been favoured so highly.
(b) Choose two areas where you disagree strongly with the preference scores shown. Consider why your perception of these areas may be so different from those of the teenagers who were surveyed.
Has the information in this Chapter changed in any way your own perception of the South West?

2 People and places

Recent trends

According to the **Official Census**, 4,326,410 people were living in the South West in 1981. Ten years earlier, there were 4,080,589. This is a difference of over 6% and, as fig. 2.1 shows, the South West ranked second (after East Anglia) for the percentage increase in a region's population during this period.

Table 3 *The natural and migrational changes in population 1971–1981 for each Standard Region in Great Britain.*

Standard Region	net natural change %	net migrational change %
Scotland	+1.2	−3.2
North	+0.5	−1.8
North West	+0.5	−3.3
Yorkshire and Humberside	+0.8	−0.9
Wales	+0.1	+2.1
West Midlands	+2.6	−1.9
East Midlands	+2.0	+2.8
East Anglia	+2.0	+9.9
South West	−0.7	+7.2
South East	+1.6	−2.8
Great Britain	+1.2	−0.6

Some of this change was due to the number of births and deaths occurring within the region during the ten years. However, we can see from Table 3 that the most important influence was **migration**. The South West was a magnet, drawing into it more people than moved out of the region. It therefore had a **net migrational gain**. This more than made up for its net loss from natural changes.

Look at the data shown in Table 3. Take each region in turn, and say whether from 1971 to 1981 that region's population showed:
- (a) a net natural loss but a net migrational gain;
- or (b) a net natural gain and also a net migrational gain;
- or (c) a net natural gain but a net migrational loss.

In each case, did the total population of the region decrease or increase? By what percentage? Check your answers with fig. 2.1.

The population changes which took place between 1971 and 1981 differed from area to area within the South West. Some parts had an overall decrease. Kennet and Purbeck (see fig. 2.8) are examples of **Rural Districts** where this occurred. A decrease in total numbers also took place in some urban areas. For example, Bath and Bournemouth each had a loss of 5%. Bristol had a 10% decrease.

The largest gain in numbers was in the District of Wimborne, where the population grew by 16,000 during the ten years. This

---

official census

A count of everyone who lives in the United Kingdom. It is done every 10 years.

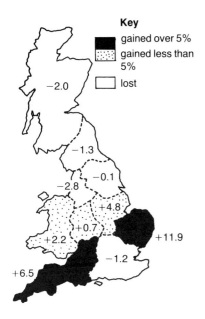

Key
- ■ gained over 5%
- ▨ gained less than 5%
- □ lost

Fig. 2.1. Population changes from 1971 to 1981 in each Region of Great Britain.

Population change has two components – (a) **natural** (births and deaths); (b) **migrational** (movement into and out of an area). Each component can have a loss or a gain. By adding or subtracting the changes within each component, we obtain a 'net' result.

To help planners make decisions, each Region is divided into Districts. These are either Urban (if they contain a large town) or Rural.

increased its total population by one third – the tenth largest percentage increase in the whole of Great Britain. Parts of east Cornwall (e.g. the District of Caradon) and SW Avon (e.g. the District of Woodspring) had very large increases – about 15%.

There are many reasons why some parts of the South West gained people while other parts lost them, but some of the geographical influences will be seen in the chapters which follow.

Changing population structure

Other changes have taken place in the population – for example in the percentage of males and females and in the number of people of different ages.

Table 4 *Percentage of each county's population in three age-groups in 1971 and 1981.*

County	1971			1981		
	0–15	16–P	over P	0–15	16–P	over P
Avon	25	58	17	21	60	19
Cornwall	22	56	22	21	57	23
Devon	22	55	23	20	57	23
Dorset	21	55	24	19	55	26
Gloucestershire	26	57	17	22	59	19
Somerset	25	56	19	22	57	21
Wiltshire	27	58	15	23	60	17
South West	24	57	19	22	57	21
Great Britain	25	59	16	22	60	18

P = pensionable age (60 for women; 65 for men)

Study Table 4 and, for each county, calculate the change from 1971 to 1981 in the percentage of people in each of the three age-groups. Which county had the lowest percentage decrease of those under 16 years old? In which county did the percentage of people of pensionable age remain the same?

As you should have discovered, most counties increased their percentage of older people. One reason for this is the attraction of the South West for retirement – possibly linked with people's perceptions of the region as a pleasant environment in which to live (Chapter 1). There was also a decrease in the number of births in the South West, so the proportion of elderly people within the region grew. The South West has the highest percentage of pensioners (21%) and the lowest percentage of under-fives (6%) of any region in the United Kingdom. In East Devon 31% of the people are pensioners; in West Dorset the figure is 25%. The national average is only 18%. Moreover, women have a longer life expectancy than men, so as the region's total population becomes more elderly, the elderly section of it becomes increasingly female. Drawing an **age/sex pyramid** is a method of showing the composition of a population by sex and age-group (the latter usually by five-year groups).

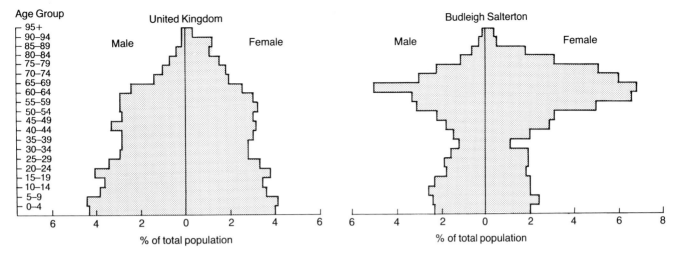

Fig. 2.2. Age/sex pyramids of the 1981 population in (a) the UK and (b) Budleigh Salterton (East Devon). In what three ways does the shape of these two pyramids differ?

New housing needs

When population numbers are increasing, there is naturally a need for more accommodation. So in the South West the building and construction industry has had a boom in employment. It has concentrated on building homes for elderly people.

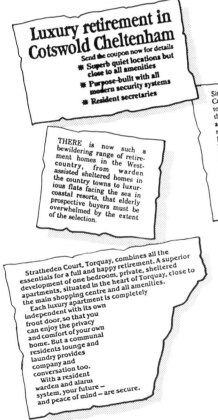

Advertisements in newspapers (fig. 2.3) show that this has usually taken two forms:
(a) converting and adapting existing property to suit the special needs of older people, e.g. internal lifts rather than stairs; one- or two-bedroomed flats rather than family-sized homes; using materials needing minimum maintenance;
(b) building new property specially for the elderly in locations close to town centres and/or with pleasant outlook and surroundings. When built in clusters with a resident warden it is known as 'sheltered housing'.

Describe the advantages which each of the special features stated in (a) and (b) above have for the elderly. What other helpful features could be included by architects and planners?

Fig. 2.3. Advertising homes built specially for the elderly.

A third type of property is also increasing in number in the South West. These are the convalescent, nursing and rest homes. Often former hotels or large private houses, they are adapted for the elderly who are non-active or in need of special care.

13

Fig. 2.4. Reporting a fear.

Show the data for one of these places by a pyramid similar in style to fig. 2.2. In what ways does its shape differ from the pyramid for Budleigh Salterton?

? Home area	? New area
job−	job+
house−	house+
friends+	friends−
sport +	sport−
environment−	environment+

Fig. 2.5. The balance of decision-making.

Fig. 2.4 spotlights a fear that if present trends continue, some places may become geriatric settlements. On the other hand, areas can benefit from this trend. For example, it brings extra employment opportunities because older people need more help in looking after their homes and to be looked after by other people.

Make a list of the extra services which an area needs to have for (a) the non-active elderly and (b) the active young retired.

Young people have also moved into the South West, to take up jobs in such booming places as Bristol and Swindon, for example. The age-sex pyramids in Table 5 reveal the results of such migration.

Table 5 *The 1981 make-up of the population of (a) Ilchester (South Somerset) and (b) the District of Thamesdown (East Wiltshire).*

	(a)		(b)	
	male	female	male	female
0–4	105	99	4920	4807
5–9	73	82	5557	5187
10–14	52	46	6208	6114
15–19	46	52	6836	6528
20–24	134	151	6223	6282
25–29	122	106	5660	5604
30–34	102	82	5850	5605
35–39	51	43	4781	4780
40–44	31	34	4425	4309
45–49	31	37	4314	4272
50–54	24	24	4345	4320
55–59	29	31	4437	4436
60–64	22	20	3442	3447
65–69	24	16	2820	3197
70–74	20	22	2205	2787
75–79	6	18	1409	2252
80–84	4	10	731	1383
85+	1	5	332	942
Total	1813		150,746	

Why move?

Migration is the response to factors which 'push' and 'pull' people. There are some things with which a likely migrant is not satisfied in the home area. Certain things in another area can attract like a magnet.

push   pull

The situation is rather like a balance. All the advantages (shown as 'pluses' in fig. 2.5) and all the disadvantages (shown as 'minuses') in the present and possible future home areas have to be weighed up. If, as in the example shown, the balance tips in favour of the future area, then the decision could be 'Let's move'.

Expanded Town

This is a settlement which existed before people were moved into it. The extra homes, shops, etc. have been added to the existing layout. (A **New Town** is one which has been built to a completely new design. An Act of Parliament has to be passed to allow it to be developed.)

For some people, moving into the South West has been a personal and **voluntary** decision – to obtain a better job, a different type of house or a pleasant environment in which to retire. For others, the move has been forced upon them, e.g. when the former Greater London Council arranged with the local authorities at Bodmin, Plymouth and Swindon to re-house people from parts of Central London which were in need of re-development. Similarly, Weston-super-Mare has re-housed people who have been moved out of Birmingham. Like the other receiving towns, it is known as an **Expanded Town**. Besides accepting people and building homes for them, growing towns need to provide enough jobs for the migrants who are of working age.

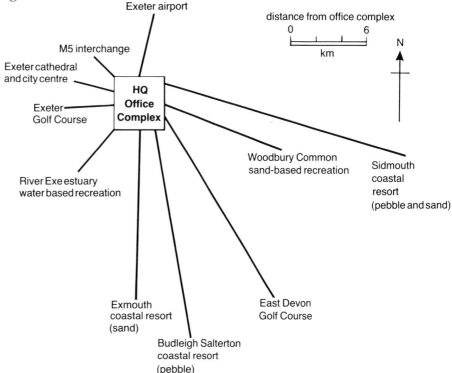

Fig. 2.6. The amenities/facilities near the London and Manchester Assurance Company Office Headquarters at Clyst St Mary, near Exeter.
What advantages does this selected location offer:
(a) an older senior executive?
(b) a younger employee with two small children?

greenfield site

A site with no previous factory or office activities; usually an area with plenty of space for future expansion and facilities for employees (e.g. car parking and sport).

Migration also takes place because owners or managers feel that it is necessary to move their firm. For example, the London and Manchester Assurance Company decided to move its headquarters away from Moorgate, central London. Many possible locations in the UK were considered, but eventually the outskirts of Exeter were chosen (fig. 2.6). Here was a **greenfield site** and a high quality environment in which to live and work. Not all employees were keen to move with the firm, and the management helped these to find alternative employment in the London area. In the end, about 100 employees moved to the South West in 1975 – 25% of the workforce at that time. In this example, migration was **forced** upon the employees. Yet they also had a choice in whether to move or stay.

Think of two or three families you know who have moved home recently. Where did they live previously? To where have they moved? Can you identify as 'push' and 'pull' factors any of the reasons why they may have moved? Were they 'voluntary' or 'forced' moves?

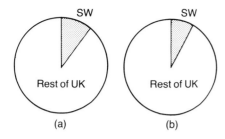

Fig. 2.7. The South West's share of the (a) area and (b) population of the United Kingdom.

pph
persons per hectare

0   50   100
└─┴─┴─┴─┴─┴─┴─┴─┴─┘
            km

Key
persons per ha

☐	0.0–0.9
░	1.0–1.9
▨	2.0–9.9
▦	10.0–19.9
■	20.0+

Densities of living

The 4 million people who live in South West England make up only 7.8% of the population of the UK (fig. 2.7). So, because it is such a large region, the average density of population is low – 1.8 persons per hectare. This contrasts with 3.5 persons per hectare for England as a whole, and with 6.1 persons per hectare for the South East region. However, within the South West there are great variations in the distribution and density of people. One half of them live in the north and east of the region (Avon, Gloucestershire and NW Wiltshire). A quarter of the total is concentrated in the Bristol–Severnside area.

Average densities range from:
0.45 pph in the District of West Somerset
and 0.56 pph in the District of North Cornwall

to   30.96 pph in the District of Plymouth
and 35.67 pph in the District of Bristol.

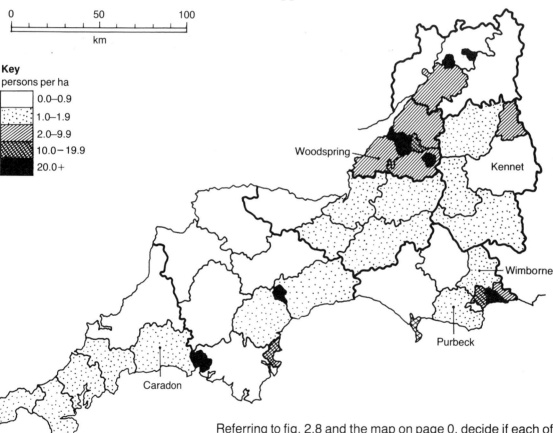

Fig. 2.8. The distribution of population and average population density in each District within the South West Standard Region. The labelled Districts are those used as examples on pages 11 and 12.

Referring to fig. 2.8 and the map on page 0, decide if each of the following statements is true or false:
(a) all areas with a density of over 20 pph are within 50 km of the coast;
(b) Cornwall has more Districts with a density of between 1.0 and 1.9 pph than any of the other six counties;
(c) Avon has no District with fewer than 2.0 pph;
(d) Dartmoor, Exmoor and the Cotswold Hills are areas with very low densities of population (fewer than 0.9 pph).

It would be a mistake, however, to match the density of population with the quality of the environment in which the people live. More important factors include the quality of design and construction of homes, also the number and the nearness of amenities which people are able to use. In many places the living environment is good, even though the density at which people are living is high. It is the duty of local authorities to approve plans for comfortable living conditions when new areas are being built or existing ones are being modernised.

Fig. 2.9 illustrates one result of 'planning for improvement'. The exclusion of traffic, the planting of shrubs, the addition of sitting-out areas for the elderly,and a play area for toddlers, have

Fig. 2.9. A part of Exeter known as Newtown.

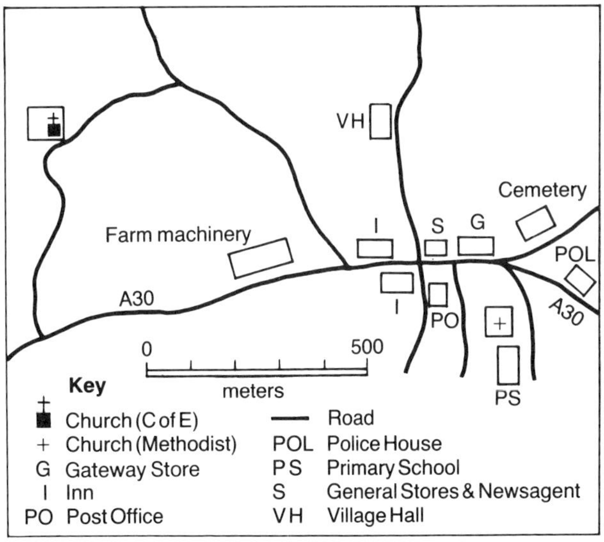

Fig. 2.10. Local needs being met within a small area at Tedburn St Mary, 10 km west of Exeter.

twilight area
In Britain, this is usually an old part of a town. It has housing of a high density which:
(a) lacks many of the basic amenities such as a bath, an inside toilet and piped cold water;
(b) has roofs, walls and paintwork in a poor state;
(c) is waiting to be developed and modernised.

helped to upgrade the living environment of a former **twilight area** close to a city centre. Amenities inside the homes have also been improved. House exteriors have been re-decorated in varying styles to make them attractive and colourful.

Communities

People live in communities. These vary in size and composition. In some smaller settlements there can be a strong community spirit. The people can be farmers or farm labourers, or can be providing the basic needs of that community. The village store/post office, public house, school and church form a central point for the people (fig. 2.10). The community is closely-knit, is often small enough for people to know each other, and depends upon the services of its members to keep it going. Many of the families have lived in the area for generations. They do not welcome change.

As settlements grow in size, people's feelings of belonging to one community become less strong. They tend to group together in different parts of the community, often with different types of housing and styles of living. Their interests become more varied,

Fig. 2.11. Poole: the three survey locations.

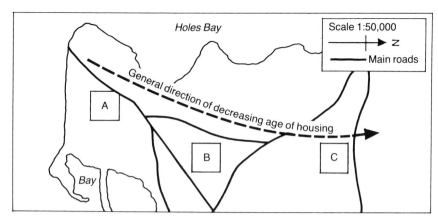

random sampling
A number of people are selected to represent the whole population. They are chosen completely by chance.

and their dependence upon one another seems less obvious. In fig. 2.11 you will see located three areas within Poole, a town of about 120,000 people. A **random sample** of 25 people living in each area was asked six questions:

1. Do you have a car?
2. How long have you been living in this home?
3. To what local clubs or groups do you belong?
4. Do you own your home, or is it rented: from the local authority or from someone else?
5. Do you work near your home, or in another part of Poole, or in another town?
6. Before you lived here, did you live nearby, or somewhere else in Poole, or in another town or village?

The person questioned was the main wage-earner in each home, and the results of the survey are shown in Table 6.

Table 6 *Answers to the six questions given by 25 people living in each of three parts of Poole.*

Question 1

	Yes	No
A	8	17
B	16	9
C	10	15

Question 2

	under 1 year	1–5 years	over 5 years
A	5	12	8
B	5	7	13
C	16	9	0

Question 3

	none	1 or 2	several
A	3	11	11
B	8	10	7
C	6	16	3

Question 4

	own	rented from another person	local authority
A	9	16	0
B	15	10	0
C	4	0	21

Question 5

	locally	same town	elsewhere
A	12	10	3
B	6	11	8
C	9	15	1

Question 6

	locally	same town	elsewhere
A	6	12	7
B	4	15	6
C	9	14	2

Put into your own words the features of the communities at A and B. Does the evidence suggest that the people living in each of the three areas have a strong feeling of belonging to a local community? What influences might help to explain the answers given to the questions in area C?

Ask the main wage-earner in your home the same six questions. Consider the answers, and decide into which of the communities A, B or C your family fits best.

Table 7 *Each region's percentage share of the foreign-born population now living in the UK.*

Born in	West Indies	India, Pakistan and Bangladesh	Africa	Canada, Australia, New Zealand	USA	Eire	rest of Europe
Region							
North	0	3	1	3	1	2	3
Yorkshire and Humberside	5	11	4	5	4	5	5
North West	5	10	6	7	7	13	7
East Midlands	6	6	8	4	3	5	4
West Midlands	14	16	6	6	3	13	6
South East	64	46	65	52	45	50	55
South West	3	3	3	8	5	4	8
East Anglia	2	1	2	3	22	1	3
Scotland	1	3	4	10	8	5	6
Wales	0	1	1	2	2	2	3
UK	100	100	100	100	100	100	100

Because these people have come from a country outside the United Kingdom, they are all known as *immigrants*.

In some towns, people from different cultural backgrounds add to the variety of a community's population. Some may have been born overseas. Others were born in Britain from parents who came from foreign countries. In Table 7 you will see that the percentage of foreign-born people living in the South West is low.

What influences may be responsible for the South West having so few foreign-born people living within it, compared to such regions as the South East, the West Midlands and the North West?

There are, however, concentrations of immigrant population in some of the older inner city areas of the region. The St Paul's Ward in Bristol (fig. 2.12) is an example. Here, 28% of the residents were born outside of the UK. The area was built mainly in the mid to late nineteenth century to house the city's rapidly growing working population. The size of the two-, three- or four-storey terraced homes has since allowed them to be sub-divided to house several families. Many have been demolished; others await urgent repair and renovation. This is in sharp contrast to the adjoining City Centre, which is newly-built, bright and prosperous.

Fig. 2.12. (a) The wards of Bristol. Note the location of St Paul's Ward in relation to the City Centre.

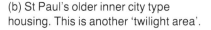

(b) St Paul's older inner city type housing. This is another 'twilight area'.

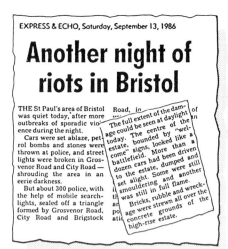

EXPRESS & ECHO, Saturday, September 13, 1986

Another night of riots in Bristol

THE St Paul's area of Bristol was quiet today, after more outbreaks of sporadic violence during the night.

Cars were set ablaze, petrol bombs and stones were thrown at police, and street lights were broken in Grosvenor Road and City Road — shrouding the area in an eerie darkness.

But about 300 police, with the help of mobile searchlights, sealed off a triangle formed by Grosvenor Road, City Road and Brigstock Road, in ...

The full extent of the damage could be seen at daylight today. The centre of the "welcome" signs, looked like a battlefield. More than a dozen cars had been driven to the estate, dumped and set alight. Some were still smouldering and another was still in full flame. Bricks, rubble and wreckage were strewn all over the concrete grounds of the high-rise estate.

Fig. 2.13. How one newspaper reported urban unrest in 1986.

Immigrants often occupy those parts of an urban area which have been left vacant as the previous residents move to the outer parts of the city (or suburbs) or to other towns. They are therefore called a **replacement population**.

On occasions, the stress of living in run-down inner city areas reaches breaking-point, and shows itself in forms of urban violence or social disorder. This happened, for example, several times in Bristol during the 1980s (fig. 2.13).

Earning their living

Many of the people living in the South West are not in paid employment because:

(a) they are too young (see Table 5);
(b) they have reached the age of retirement (see fig. 2.2);
(c) although they are of working age, they cannot find a job (see fig. 1.8);
(d) they are caring for young children or elderly parents full-time.

38% of the region's population are in paid employment, and you can see in Table 8 a way of grouping their activities. Since 1980, employees have been divided into these ten official Groups. This is known as the **Standard Industrial Classification**.

Table 8 *How people (male and female together) were employed in the United Kingdom and the South West in June 1987.*

Employment Groups	UK %	South West Number (approx)	South West %
0 Agriculture, forestry, fishing	1.6	48,000	2.8
1 Energy and water supply	3.1	26,000	1.9
2 Metals, minerals and chemicals	5.0	46,000	2.8
3 Metal goods, engineering and vehicle production	14.6	194,000	13.8
4 Other manufactures	11.8	142,000	11.0
5 Construction	5.3	65,000	5.3
6 Distribution, hotels and catering	18.4	357,000	22.4
7 Transport and communication	6.4	84,000	5.4
8 Banking, finance and insurance	7.1	146,000	6.7
9 Public administration and other	26.7	490,000	27.8
Totals	100.0	1,598,000	100.0

Which of these Groups do you consider provide a 'service' activity? Put into rank order of decreasing percentage the Groups in each of (a) the UK; (b) the South West. In what ways does the employment structure of the South West differ from that of the United Kingdom?

3 Contrasting landscapes

The South West attracts many holiday-makers. One reason for this is the variety of its scenery, which makes the landscape interesting and appealing. In Chapter 7 we shall look at tourism, but in this chapter we investigate the major landforms of the region. To explain the physical landscape we need to ask the following questions:

(a) How does the type of rock affect the form or appearance of the landscape?
(b) What do we know about the effects of weathering and erosion processes which are acting on the rock? Do these processes explain the landforms we can see?
(c) Are there any features of the landscape which we cannot explain by studying the rocks and the processes of weathering and erosion? Do we have to look into the past to find the reasons?
(d) Has human activity had important effects on the physical landscape?

Fig. 3.1. The geology of South West England.

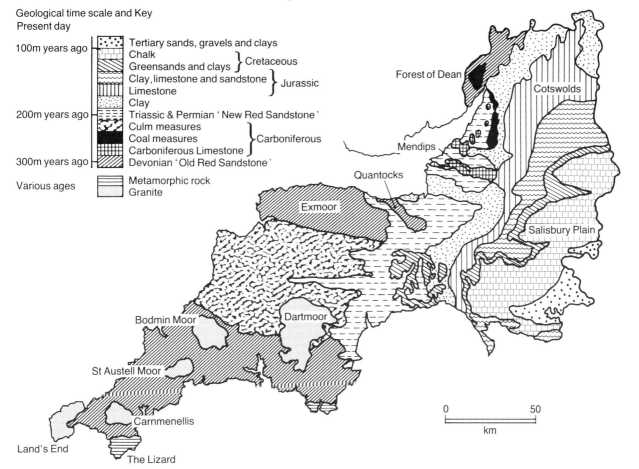

Geological time scale and Key
Present day

100m years ago

Tertiary sands, gravels and clays
Chalk
Greensands and clays } Cretaceous
Clay, limestone and sandstone } Jurassic
Limestone
Clay

200m years ago

Triassic & Permian 'New Red Sandstone'
Culm measures
Coal measures } Carboniferous
Carboniferous Limestone

300m years ago

Devonian 'Old Red Sandstone'

Various ages

Metamorphic rock
Granite

Fig. 3.2. Dartmoor landscape. Tors stand on top of the ridges which rise up from broad hollows or basins. Boulders lie on the slopes below the tors. ▶

Fig. 3.3. Dartmoor tor. The granite blocks are divided by vertical and horizontal joints, which are opened out by weathering.

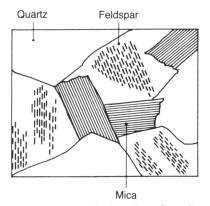

Fig. 3.4. A magnified section of granite. This shows crystals of the three minerals which make up most of the rock.

A granite upland

Dartmoor is part of a huge mass of granite, an **igneous rock** which lies beneath the surface westward to Land's End. Where it protrudes through the cover of sedimentary rocks, as it does in Bodmin Moor and Dartmoor, the granite forms higher ground because of its hardness.

Around the granite is a narrow ring of **metamorphic rock**, called an aureole, which forms the outer edges of the upland.

The Dartmoor plateau is not flat but varies in height from 250 m around the edges to a maximum of 605 m at High Willhays, the highest point in Southern England. The moorland surface dips into shallow basins and valleys and swells upwards to form ridges and hills (fig. 3.2). In places the smooth slopes are broken by steps, separating broad terraces of flatter ground. On many of the hill summits are grey granite blocks called tors. In the broad basins between the hills, peat bogs have formed. They are the source of many rivers which radiate from Dartmoor in all directions. Streams have cut shallow valleys in the resistant granite, but at the edge of the moor they flow in deep gorges.

How much of this landscape can be explained by the rock in which it is formed? Dartmoor is higher than the surrounding areas because of granite's physical strength or hardness. But granite does weather and decay. (See figs. 3.3 and 3.4.) The formation of the hills and ridges is also influenced by the character of the granite. In some places the vertical joints are close together, so that the rock has a close network of cracks running through it. There it is weaker, more easily weathered and has been eroded into valleys by streams. Where the joints are more widely spaced the granite is more resistant to erosion and stands up as hills which separate the broad marshy valleys. The rivers are more powerful lower down their courses, where they reach the margins of the moor. Many small tributaries have brought an increased volume of water and the gradient is much steeper, and the rivers have cut deep valleys back into the rim of Dartmoor. The character of granite and the weathering and river erosion help to explain the Dartmoor landscape. But more information is still needed, and for this we must look into the past.

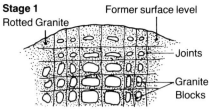

Stage 1
Rotted Granite — Former surface level
Joints
Granite Blocks

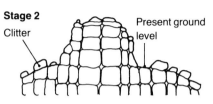

Stage 2
Clitter — Present ground level

Fig. 3.5. The chemical weathering theory of tor formation. The climate of Britain has changed many times in the past. In a hot, wet climate the rainwater would attack granite more quickly, mainly along the joints. Rotted, weathered material would surround blocks of solid granite (Stage 1). Later, probably in the Ice Age, when the ground was frozen, the loose material and broken rock slid into the valleys. The solid blocks which remained formed tors. The boulders which lie around the tors are called clitters (Stage 2).

Key
a Granite tor
b 'Avenue' tor
c Site of tor destroyed by erosion
d Clitter
e Basin filled with weathered material
f Old erosion surface
g Close jointing in granite
h Wide jointing in granite
i Gorge on edge of granite

Fig. 3.7. Model diagram of a Dartmoor landscape.

Use the cut-away side of the model to draw a cross-section. Some of the features on this section have been identified for you. Label these on your copy and add more labels to show: tors, clitters, ancient erosion surfaces.

National Parks
These were created after an Act of Parliament was passed in 1949. Although much of the land is privately owned, there are large areas to which people have access for recreation and enjoyment.

Although they are being attacked by physical and chemical weathering, the tors are not the result of processes which are happening now. In fact, they are still a bit of a mystery. Two theories used to explain them are shown in figs. 3.5 and 3.6.

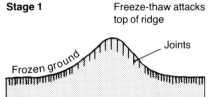

Stage 1
Freeze-thaw attacks top of ridge
Joints
Frozen ground

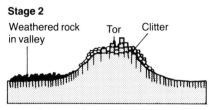

Stage 2
Weathered rock in valley — Tor — Clitter

Fig. 3.6. The mechanical weathering theory of tor formation. In the Ice Age, when Dartmoor had a cold climate, freeze-thaw weathering attacked the tops of ridges (Stage 1). This opened up the joints and pushed blocks of granite sideways, so that some slipped down into the valleys (Stage 2).

Which of these two theories is the better explanation is difficult to decide. Both theories involve the Ice Age, when Dartmoor was a tundra region. Certainly the floors of the broad hollows are filled with rock debris which slid or was washed down the frozen slopes. Layers of peat have now been formed in these basins.

There are many flat areas of ground which form broad platforms at two heights above sea-level. These are shown in fig. 3.7. How were these platforms produced?

It is thought that the flat surfaces show that Dartmoor has twice been worn away to an almost completely flat plain. The highest level was formed in the very distant past. The lower level is younger. Today these levels are being destroyed by erosion.

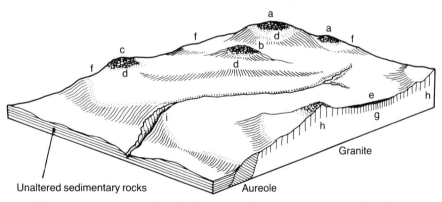

Unaltered sedimentary rocks — Aureole — Granite

Compared with geological time, it is only very recently that people have affected the physical landscape of the moor. Miners of tin and copper tore into the surface soil and rocks, leaving rough, hummocky ground. Quarrying of granite, china clay and other rocks leaves great holes and waste material.

Tourists tramp around the beauty spots so that paths become eroded into gullies. The Ministry of Defence uses large areas of the moor for training. Vehicles cut up the surface and in the firing ranges the ground is pock-marked with shell craters. Reservoirs have been built in several valleys, changing the flow of the rivers. Compared to the size of the moor, with its great hills and broad, peat-filled basins, many of the effects of human activity are small. But they change the appearance of the landscape and cause arguments about damage being done within a **National Park**.

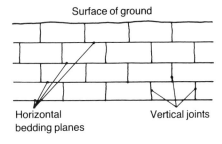

Fig. 3.8. The system of joints in Carboniferous Limestone. These are cracks into which water can seep.

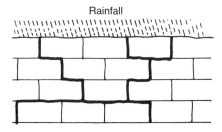

Fig. 3.9. Chemical weathering. Rainwater is a weak acid which dissolves calcium carbonate which makes up the limestone. When the rain flows along the joints and bedding planes it widens them by this chemical action. Tunnels are formed along which underground streams flow.

Fig. 3.10. Model diagram of the landscape of the Mendip Hills.

Make a copy of the diagram and label these features: a low hill formed of sandstone; the flat plateau surface; a swallet into which a stream flows; a small hollow caused by solution of the limestone; the gorge; a dry valley.

A limestone upland

The Mendip Hills rise sharply from the low Somerset Plain like a great wall, 30 km long. Most of the surface is a level plateau between 250 m and 300 m above sea-level with few low hills rising another 30 m higher. On the southern edge erosion has cut deep valleys, the best known being Cheddar Gorge with cliffs 100 m high. Most of the Mendips plateau is formed from hard carboniferous limestone and it is this rock which explains some of the main features, both above and below ground.

Rain falling on the limestone surface passes downwards into the rock and does not flow across the surface. The plateau is therefore dry, with few streams to be found. This helps to explain the flatness, for there is no vigorous river erosion to cut valleys into the surface. In some places, however, there are shallow hollows in the surface caused in two ways. Either:
(a) the limestone dissolves in rainwater, gradually making the depressions deeper and wider; or
(b) shallow caves collapse, and the roof falls into the hole.

In a few places older rocks, which generally are hidden beneath the limestone, appear at the surface. The hardest of these is a sandstone, which produces the higher areas rising above the flat plateau surface (figs. 3.10 and 3.11). Around these low sandstone hills there are layers of shale, which is softer than either the sandstone or the limestone. But the sandstone and shale are not permeable and rainfall forms streams which flow onto the limestone. Once they reach the limestone they disappear down widened joints called swallets. This causes the underground drainage of the Mendip Hills.

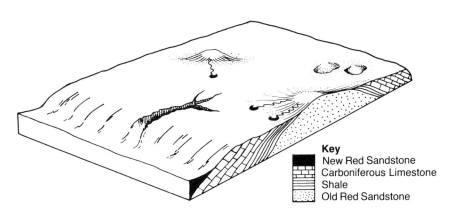

Key
New Red Sandstone
Carboniferous Limestone
Shale
Old Red Sandstone

The geology of the Mendips helps to explain some of the landforms. The surface of the limestone is weathered chemically, but this is a very slow process and so this hard, permeable rock stands up above the younger rocks.

The great gorge at Cheddar, shown in fig. 3.11, needs further explanation. During the Ice Age the joints in the limestone at ground level were blocked, probably with ice. In summer the snow on the surface thawed, but the meltwater could not escape into the frozen ground beneath. Large volumes of water then flowed across the limestone plateau, cutting deeply downwards into the edge. Now, with the soil and surface rock no longer

Fig. 3.11. Cheddar Gorge. Although it is dry today, the gorge shows the power of running water, which eroded deeply into the edge of the Mendips plateau. A road runs along the bottom of the gorge and cars give you an idea of scale. The beds of limestone are tilted downwards to the left of the photograph. Because of this tilt the right side of the gorge is sloping but the left side is vertical. In the distance is the Somerset Plain, formed of sandstone and clays.

differential erosion
Each type of rock has a different character or make-up. For example, some rocks are more resistant to weathering and erosion and therefore they usually form higher ground or coastal headlands. The differences in relief or surface shape of the land are mainly caused in this way.

Fig. 3.12. The Mendips plateau. A low hill of Old Red Sandstone rises above the surface of the Carboniferous Limestone. This surface is the result of erosion over many millions of years.

frozen, the rainwater has returned to the underground caves and passages. These have been enlarged by chemical weathering and by streams to form the great cave systems of the Mendips.

There are two landscape features of the Mendips shown on fig. 3.10 which have not been explained, although you may be able to suggest the formation of the most obvious one.

The steep escarpment at the edge of the plateau is formed by **differential erosion**. The limestone has withstood erosion because of its hardness, whilst the softer New Red Sandstone and clays have been worn down. The steepness of the limestone edge is caused by the same vertical jointing and strength which explains the high cliffs at Cheddar Gorge.

The second feature is the largest in area and yet it is the least noticeable. The broad flat plateau surface is the product of very ancient erosion, when the carboniferous limestone was slowly worn down over many millions of years. Geologists believe that this very old plain was then covered by the deposition of younger rocks. These rocks have now been removed by erosion to expose the flat surface which was formed long ago.

In more recent times human activity has caused minor erosion in many parts of the Mendip Hills. Numerous pits and waste-heaps are evidence of centuries of lead mining. Today the limestone is a source of roadstone and is also used in the steel and cement industries. Huge quarries at several places along the edge of the plateau have opened up the rock strata (see fig. 4.12).

Fig. 3.13. Scarp slope on the edge of Salisbury Plain. The gullies running down the slope were probably caused by meltwater when this part of Britain had a climate much colder than today's. The terraces at the base of the slope were built by early farmers.

Fig. 3.14. Salisbury Plain. The almost flat skyline and the level heights of the ridges are evidence that this is another example of an old erosion surface.

Fig. 3.15. Dry valley on Salisbury Plain.

Chalklands and scarplands

In the east of the region a large area of chalk rock forms much of the surface. These are the upland areas of Salisbury Plain, the Marlborough Downs and the Dorset Downs, shown on the map (fig. 3.33). The edges of these uplands form steep scarp slopes overlooking the surrounding lowlands (fig. 3.13).

The largest chalkland area, Salisbury Plain, is a plateau with an undulating surface of broad, ridges separated by valleys which are often deep and steep-sided. The view across Salisbury Plain shows an almost flat surface, because the ridge-tops reach roughly the same height and the valleys are hidden between them.

Few of the valleys have permanent streams flowing along them, because the chalk is very permeable, allowing rain to sink quickly into the rock. There are therefore few rivers to erode the surface and this is the reason why chalk forms higher ground, even though it is physically softer than many other rocks. It also helps to explain the steepness of the scarp slopes at the edge of the Plain, for there is little erosion by water running down the slopes. The vertical joints in the chalk are another reason.

Yet there are valleys on the chalklands and, although most of them are dry today (fig. 3.15), they have been eroded by streams. When were these valleys formed? Fig. 3.16 shows two theories.

1. Erosion of a chalkland valley in a wet climate in the past

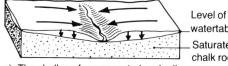 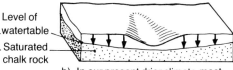

a) The chalk surface cannot absorb all the rain. Some flows across the surface to form a stream.

b) In our present drier climate most rain soaks into the ground. The water-table is below the floor of the valley, which is therefore dry.

2. Erosion of a chalkland valley in a cold climate in the past

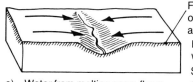 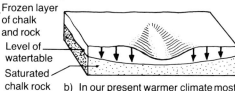

a) Water from melting snow flows across the frozen surface to form a stream.

b) In our present warmer climate most rain soaks into the ground. The water-table is below the floor of the valley, which is therefore dry.

Fig. 3.16. Two different explanations of dry valleys.

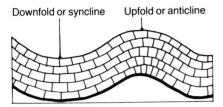

Fig. 3.17. Folding in chalk beds.

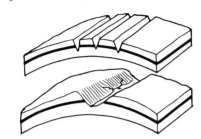

Fig. 3.18. Where the rocks are stretched along the top of an anticline the joints are opened up. This weakens the rock which is more easily eroded. A valley may then be formed where there was once an upfold.

A few valleys have been eroded deeply enough to reach the water-table (or zone of permanently saturated rock) and here streams flow all year. But the level of the water-table in the chalk rises each winter, when the autumn and winter rains have had time to percolate down through the rock. This causes streams to flow, usually from January to June, in some of the valleys which are dry for the rest of the year when the level of the water-table falls again.

The beds of chalk are often folded (fig. 3.17). This was caused by earth movements about 30 million years ago. The Vale of Pewsey on the northern side of Salisbury Plain, and the Vale of Wardour on the west, have been formed where the chalk was folded upwards. You might expect an anticline or upfold to produce a range of hills rather than a valley. The explanation is to be found in 3.18 and 3.19. Older layers of rock, once hidden beneath the chalk, have been exposed by erosion of the crest of the anticline. The differences in the outcrops of rocks produce the varied scenery of the Vale of Wardour, shown in fig 3.19.

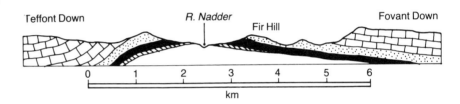

Fig. 3.19. Cross-section through the Vale of Wardour. The valley of the River Nadder has been eroded into the anticline. The edges of the chalk and Greensand form escarpments on each side of the valley.

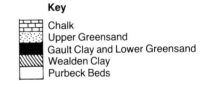

Key

Chalk
Upper Greensand
Gault Clay and Lower Greensand
Wealden Clay
Purbeck Beds

So far in this chapter we have studied three areas: a granite upland; a limestone plateau; a chalkland. To analyse the differences in these areas, copy out the following table and record information about the landscape.

3.20. *Comparison of three contrasting landscapes.*

	Dartmoor	Mendip Hills	Salisbury Plain
Landscape and main landforms			
Influence of rocks on landscape			
Weathering and erosion processes affecting the landscape now			
Erosion processes which have affected the landscapes in the past			

Fig. 3.21. The sandspit of Dawlish Warren stretches for 2 km across the mouth of the Exe Estuary. At high tide it has a maximum width of 400 m but at low tide, when the beach and mudflats are uncovered, it is about 1 km at its widest point.

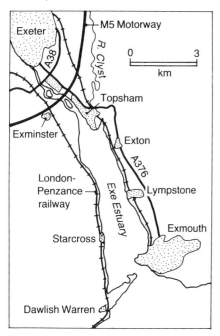

Fig. 3.22. Dawlish Warren and the estuary of the River Exe.

Fig. 3.23. Model diagram showing a cross-section of Dawlish Warren and the six zones which make up the sandspit. The arrows show some of the processes which are acting on the sandspit.

When you have read this page and the next you should be able to explain the five processes shown by the arrows.

nature reserve
An area of land or water which is managed to conserve wildlife. This usually means that the habitats of plants and animals need to be protected.

Site of Special Scientific Interest
An area can be called this if it has plants, animals or geology which are unusual and important. The government decides which areas should be classed as SSSIs.

Coastal landforms: a sandspit

Although it rises only a few metres above sea-level, the sandspit of Dawlish Warren has been formed by the accumulation of many millions of tons of sand over the last 5,000 years. At low tide its surface is made up of six zones, shown in fig. 3.23.

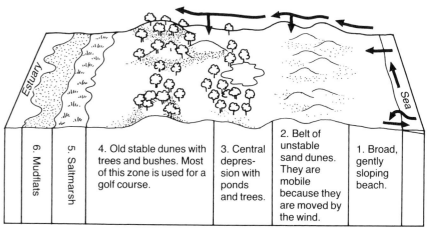

Each zone provides a different environment for wildlife and a great variety of plants is found on the Warren. Because some of these species can exist only in special conditions and are not common elsewhere, most of the sandspit is a **Nature Reserve** and a **Site of Special Scientific Interest**. So too is a large area of the estuary where flocks of wading birds and wildfowl feed and roost on the salt marsh and mud flats (zones 5 and 6 in fig. 3.23).

Dawlish Warren today is the result of three physical processes:

1. Wave action.

(a) Waves approach the beach head-on and the swash pushes sand up the beach. The waves which break gently on the beach are constructive. Large storm waves, crashing on to the beach in rapid succession, have a more powerful backwash. The effect is destructive, carrying sand back into the sea. Fig. 3.24 shows the differences between these two waves.

(b) Waves driven by the prevailing winds from the south west move the sand along the beach. This movement is like a conveyor belt carrying sand along the coast from west to east, and is called longshore drift (fig. 3.24).

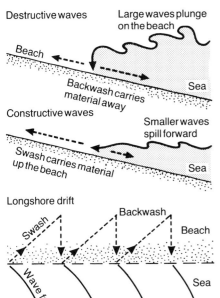

Fig. 3.24. Two types of waves and longshore drift.

Fig. 3.25. The roots of marram grass anchor the sand. Its stems and leaves trap sand blown inland by the wind, but it can be killed by trampling feet.

Fig. 3.26. The western end of Dawlish Warren.

Make a list of each of the methods of protection shown. Explain the purpose of each method.

(c) Waves from the south east run into the rivermouth, carrying sand round into the shape of a hook. This also happens when a strong tidal current flows into the estuary.

2. Wind action.
Onshore winds blow sand off the beach onto the dunes (zone 2) and some is trapped by marram grass leaves (fig. 3.25).

3. River deposition
The River Exe carries silt into the estuary, depositing it on the mud-banks and salt-marsh.

Although Dawlish Warren is geologically very young its future has been in danger for at least 200 years. The seaward face has been eroded by over one metre a year, making the beach and Outer Warren narrower. At times storm waves have broken right through the Warren, threatening its complete destruction.

Why have destructive processes become dominant? The answer begins long ago.
(a) For thousands of years the River Exe has deposited sediment close to the coastline.
(b) Increasing temperatures at the end of the Ice Age raised the sea to its present level about 5,000 years ago. This has allowed waves to move the sediment back to the coast and to erode further the cliffs in South Devon. These two processes produced the sand to build Dawlish Warren.
(c) Today the sediment carried by the river is not enough. The railway and sea wall built in 1848 reduced cliff erosion to the west, whilst a breakwater built at Langstone Rock stopped sand moving by longshore drift eastwards to the Warren.

The beach has become lower and narrower as sand supplies decreased. Now waves break closer inshore, damaging the dunes, which are also trampled by holidaymakers. This kills the vegetation, exposing loose sand to the wind. Fig. 3.26 shows the protection programme carried out in the 1970s to reduce the effect of these different erosion processes.

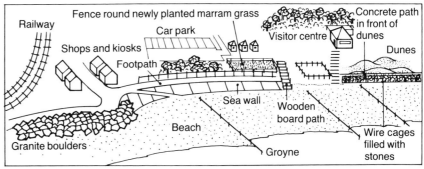

The Nature Reserve Warden makes decisions about the way different habitats on the Reserve should be managed and also provides information to people visiting Dawlish Warren.

What would the Warden want people to learn from a visit to the Centre? Make a list of the kinds of information you would expect to see displayed. Are there any things people are asked not to do, in order to protect the Warren and its wildlife?

Bays and headlands

The geology map of the coast of the Isle of Purbeck in Dorset (fig. 3.27) shows clearly the effect of differential erosion, where the sea has eroded the weaker rocks more than the resistant ones.

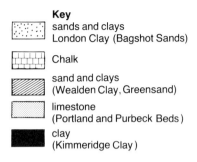

Fig. 3.27. Simplified geology of the Isle of Purbeck.

Key

sands and clays
London Clay (Bagshot Sands)

Chalk

sand and clays
(Wealden Clay, Greensand)

limestone
(Portland and Purbeck Beds)

clay
(Kimmeridge Clay)

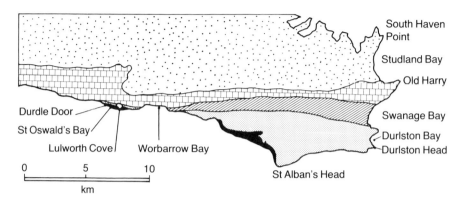

In fig. 3.27 we can see that the eastern sides of the main headlands are formed of chalk and limestone, which are more resistant. The weaker sands and clays have been eroded into large bays at Swanage and Studland. Along this stretch the rocks run at right angles to the coastline.

West from Durlston Head the plan or shape of the coastline changes because the beds of rock now run almost parallel to the coast. There is a second important geological change as we go westwards from St Alban's Head to Lulworth Cove. The beds become tilted, so that the layers of Portland and Purbeck limestone are much narrower (see fig. 3.28).

The folding which tilted these beds also cracked them in places, and waves have attacked these weaknesses. So the beds of limestone, which form the edge of the coast, have been broken through. The broad bays of Mupe and Worbarrow show the result, but the most spectacular example is at Lulworth Cove.

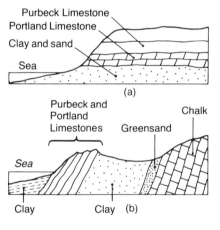

Fig. 3.28. Geological cross-sections (a) near St Alban's Head (b) near Lulworth Cove.

Fig. 3.29. Lulworth Cove, looking along the coastline from east to west.

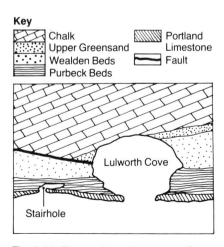

Fig. 3.30. The geology of Lulworth Cove.

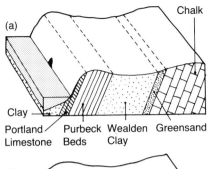

(a)

Chalk

Clay

Portland Limestone | Purbeck Beds | Wealden Clay | Greensand

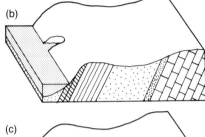

(b)

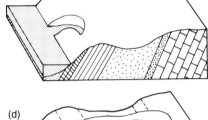

(c)

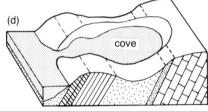

(d)

cove

Fig. 3.31. Stages in the formation of Lulworth Cove.

Trace or draw a sketch of fig. 3.29 and copy the information shown on it. Add these measurements to your drawing:

  width of cove (E to W): 500 m;
  depth of cove (mouth to chalk cliffs): 350 m;
  height of limestone cliffs at mouth of cove: 30 m.

Use arrows and labels to show: St Oswald's Bay, Durdle Door.
Using fig. 3.30 show on your drawing by means of labels:

  Limestone, which forms the lips of the Cove;
  Wealden Clays, which form the lower cliffs on either side of the Cove;
  Greensands.

Once wave-erosion had broken through the outer barrier of limestone, it began to attack the softer clays and sands. These were eroded more quickly. The stages in the formation of Lulworth Cove are shown in fig. 3.31. (c) shows Stair Hole today.

Copy fig. 3.31 (a)–(d) and write notes against each to explain what is happening.

Although the erosive force of the sea is greatest on the outer cliffs of limestone, which are exposed to the strongest waves, Lulworth Cove is still getting larger. Waves which approach from the SW, S or SE can pass through the entrance. By looking at an atlas map we can see that the furthest distance winds can blow without interruption by any land, is from the SW across the Atlantic. Waves from this direction are usually very powerful.

Inside the cove, storm waves attack the base of the cliffs, undercutting them and causing boulders of chalk and limestone to crash down. The waves also sort out and grade the material which forms the beach. Sand and fine shingle are found on the western side and the shingle gets larger as you walk along the beach to the east. Other processes, besides the waves, are also involved in the cliff erosion:

(a) Rainwater attacks the chalk, limestone and sandstone chemically.

(b) Running water washes loose material down the cliff face and causes gullying. Small valleys have been cut into the clays. The largest of these has formed along a geological fault, which has further weakened the beds of clay.

(c) Rainwater, seeping down into the beds of clay, causes the lower layers to soften, so that they slump onto the beach.

(d) Where erosion is very active, rock is continually falling down. But in places the cliffs are being worn back more slowly and vegetation has a chance to establish itself.

  Although plant roots can hold loose soil together they also penetrate into cracks and joints, widening them and helping to break up the rocks.

(e) The fame of Lulworth Cove's scenery attracts many tourists. One summer's afternoon there were 290 cars and 3 coaches in the car park. These probably meant at least 700 visitors. Most visitors walk around the bay and along the coast nearby. The effect can be seen in the paths that have been worn.

Use the information in the last four paragraphs to add more detail to your sketch of Lulworth Cove. Your completed drawing should provide an explanation of how geology and the processes of erosion have shaped this stretch of coast.

The major landforms of the South West

Most of the landscape of the region consists of higher ground which is shaped into plateaus and escarpments. These are located on fig. 3.32 and can be put into separate groups.

(a) Dartmoor, the largest area of land over 400 metres, together with the lower plateaus of Bodmin Moor, St Austell Moor, Carnmenellis and Land's End.

(b) Exmoor, with its broad, flat-topped ridges separated by deep valleys, and the Quantock Hills.

(c) the table-flat hills of East Devon and West Dorset, between which run the valleys of the River Sid and the River Axe.

(d) Salisbury Plain and the other gently rolling, low plateaus of the Marlborough Downs and Dorset Heights.

(e) the Mendip Hills.

(f) the long escarpment of the Cotswold Hills with its steep scarp slope to the Severn Vale.

Surrounding these higher hills are lower plateaus into which the coastline has been cut. The edges of these lower plateaus produce great cliffs and headlands. Between these rocky stretches are the valleys and estuaries of the Exe, Tamar, Torridge and Taw rivers.

There are two large areas of lowland:

(a) the valley and flood-plain of the River Severn, between the Cotswold Hills on the east and the hills of the Forest of Dean to the west.

(b) the very flat, low-lying Somerset Levels, which form a broad plain between the Quantock and Mendip Hills.

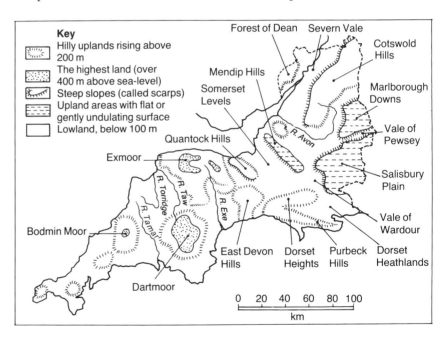

Fig. 3.32. The major landforms of South West England.

1. Make a list of the areas of higher ground named on the map (fig. 3.32). Now compare that map with fig. 3.1 and match the rock type with these uplands. You should have six types of rock in your second list.

2. Which rocks are found in the lowland areas of Somerset and the Severn Vale?

4 Using natural resources

natural resources
These occur in or on the earth and are exploited to meet human needs. They are therefore sources of economic wealth and include things like: soil in which food is grown; rocks and metal ores which are quarried or mined; water, which is obtained from beneath the surface or collected and stored in reservoirs; and fish, which are harvested from the sea. Some natural resources are important because they provide beautiful scenery which is economically valuable to the tourist industry.

Fig. 4.1. Rough ground, disused water channels and stone ruins mark the site of an old tin mine on Dartmoor. They provide a habitat which the ring ousel, a rare bird, finds attractive for breeding. In this case it could be argued that damage to the landscape has benefited wildlife. ▶

derelict land
This is land which has been badly damaged and neglected so that it would not be useful without treatment. Abandoned railways and the sites of old extractive and manufacturing industries are some examples.
  In order of total area of derelict land, the English counties worst affected are:
1. Cornwall
2. Greater Manchester
3. Lancashire
4. West Yorkshire
5. Derbyshire
6. Greater London
  Much of Cornwall's 5,000 hectares of derelict land is old mineral workings which have blended into the landscape over time. Only 12% is thought to be worth reclaiming.

Most of the goods and services we need in our daily lives, including our food, involve the use of **natural resources** and the landscape shows the effect of this in many ways.

Farming and forestry are the two industries which have most influenced the appearance of the countryside we see today. The South West did not experience the development of large urban and industrial areas based on coal-mining. But it would be wrong to think that the only important resources are its soil and scenery, and that agriculture and tourism are the only important economic activities. Fishing has always been a significant occupation and there are many small harbours, especially along the Devon and Cornwall coasts. A close look at the landscape in many parts of the region would also show you evidence that the exploitation of mineral resources has left many areas of **derelict land**.

Often the scars of past exploitation have become hidden by vegetation, and the sides of waste-heaps rounded by erosion. But the clues are still there, embedded in the general appearance of the landscape and the effects, visible or invisible, remain (see fig. 1.5). Resource development often causes changes to the ecosystem. For example, the removal of a woodland or the damming of a stream destroys or changes the habitat and therefore the wildlife. Look at fig. 4.1, however.

The exploitation of resources causes many arguments between those who wish to preserve the landscape in its present state and those who see the opportunities to create economic activity and wealth. In this chapter we look at these arguments, using the mining and water supply industries as examples. Since nearly 50,000 people in the South West are employed in forestry, fishing and farming, and over 10,000 in mining, the resources to be found in the rocks, the soil and the sea are vital to the health of the region's economy. So too is the scenery, because it is the basis of the tourist industry. Chapter 5 deals with farming and the ways it affects life in the countryside.

Table 10 *Value of main minerals produced in the UK in 1986 (in £ millions).*

Petroleum	8883
Coal	4602
Natural gas	2508
Sand and gravel	420
Limestone and chalk	420
China clay	183
Igneous rock	163
Salt	70
Potash	50
Sandstone	49
Industrial sand	35
Clay and shale	21
Gypsum and anhydrite	20
Tin	19

Fig. 4.2. Mineral workings and main underground water supplies.

Using the rocks

There is a rich variety of useful minerals in the South West. Some, such as tin and copper, have been mined for centuries and the richest deposits are exhausted. There are no large coalfields but there is an important oilfield, and rocks like limestone provide industrial minerals, especially for the construction industries. Although these minerals are often of low value per tonne they are mined in very large quantities. The quarries are widely spread in order to reduce transport costs to centres of population, road-building sites, etc.

The location of mineral deposits and therefore of mines and quarries, is determined by the geological history of the region.

1. Using fig. 4.2 and the geology map (fig. 3.1)
   (a) identify the parent rocks and name the areas from which
      (i) limestone, (ii) sand and gravel are obtained.
   (b) find the links between rock type and the deposits of (i) tin, copper and wolfram, (ii) china clay.
2. Which parts of the South West have few mines or quarries? Which rocks form the landscape in these areas?

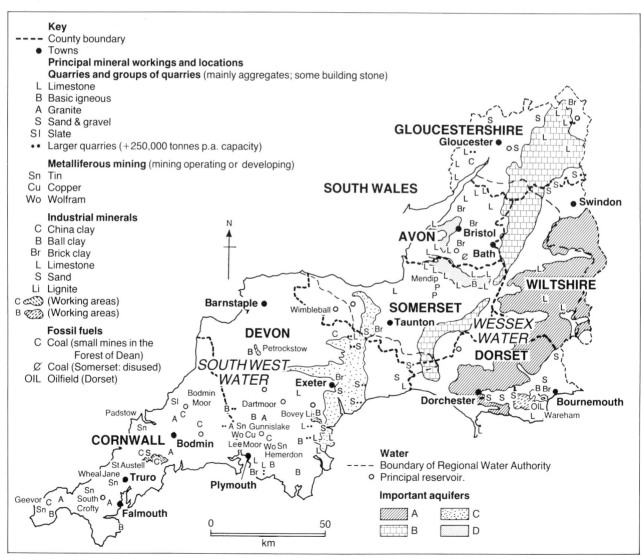

34

Table 11 *Cornish tin output in tonnes.*

1967	1422
1972	3279
1977	3857
1982	4174
1983	4067
1984	5047
1985	5204
1986	4067

Table 12 *World tin prices per tonne (in £s).*

1977	6196
1982	7282
1983	8761
1984	9238
1985	8304
1986	4000

RTZ to axe 1,000 jobs at Cornish tin mines

By Andrew Cornelius in London, and Graham Smith in Cornwall

The Cornish tin mining industry pleaded for Government support after more than 1,000 miners were issued with redundancy notices. Three mines owned by Rio Tinto-Zinc, the multinational mining group, will shut on August 1 unless the Government provides between £20 million and £30 million.

Fig. 4.3. West Cornwall in the news.

Fig. 4.4. The cycle of metal prices and production.

Make a copy of the diagram. Between the boxes, where you think they fit best, put these 3 labels:
(a) less exploration for new ore deposits;
(b) increased production;
(c) some mines forced to close.

Tin mining: problems of prices and jobs

Tin ore occurs in the granite of West Cornwall in narrow veins and is mined in deep shafts. It has been mined for centuries and the ruins of the engine-houses mark the sites of abandoned mines. (See fig. 1.5.) Although the ore has a very low metal content, the high price of tin has meant that since the 1960s a few of the old mines have been re-worked and new veins explored. In 1979 a new mine was started at Wheal Concord and Wheal Jane was re-opened. With the mines at Geevor, South Crofty and Pendarves the area then produced 40% of the tin Britain needed, worth £57m each year. These mines are shown in fig. 4.2. Employment at the mines provided £16m annually in wages, £6m was paid to local suppliers for goods and services and £0.6m in local rates and taxes.

Most of the world's tin comes from South East Asia and South America, where production costs are often much lower than in Cornwall. In Cornwall the depth of the mines produces drainage problems and the ore is low in metal content. Cornish tin mining therefore requires a high price for tin of around £7,000 a tonne to make a profit. Because the economies of some Third World countries are dependent on primary products like tin, an arrangement for controlling prices has been in operation. One agreement between the major producers and consumers has meant that much tin is bought by a central agency and then re-sold. During the 1970s and early 1980s the world price of tin continued to rise, even though there was a fall in demand because of the general economic recession and through the use of cheaper aluminium to make cans. The world price in tin was tied to the value of the American dollar. As this value increased so did tin prices but when, in 1985, the dollar lost value, the market price of tin collapsed (see Table 12). There were now large stocks of tin which had been bought at prices higher than those at which they could be re-sold.

The result of the price collapse was the closure of several Cornish mines, including that at Geevor. If a mine closes and maintenance and pumping of water cease, the cost of repairing the damage may be too high to allow re-opening. For the mining villages of West Cornwall, already an area of high unemployment, the low tin prices are a serious threat. Their social and economic welfare depends upon factors which are international, and well beyond their control. But the situation was not a new one. The cycle of high and low prices is typical of many metals, bringing periods of prosperity and depression to mining areas in many parts of the world.

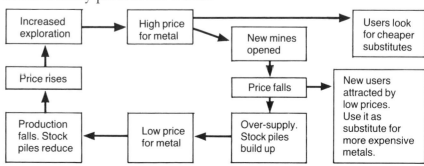

uses of tungsten

As it is very hard and withstands high temperatures, it is used for light bulb filaments, television tubes, the cutting edge of machine tools and high speed drills and for armour-piercing projectiles.

strategic minerals

These are materials which are essential for military forces to operate and for a nation's manufacturing industry to function. Countries like Britain stockpile reserves of these materials, especially if home-production is small and if the main producing countries might not be close allies in a future war.

Fig. 4.5. Site plan for the new tungsten mine at Hemerdon. In full operation the mine would have a big effect on the landscape, especially on Crownhill Down. The waste would be dumped here, covering the ruins of prehistoric settlements and ancient tin workings. Agricultural land would be lost, though most of it is of poor quality. The villages of Hemerdon and Sparkwell, several farms and cottages, are close to the mine-site. Rock blasting, excavation, crushing and transport of millions of tons of rock would cause noise, vibration, dust and increased traffic on the roads. Houses would lose value and some would have to be demolished. The mining company has promised to pay compensation to people most affected.

Fig. 4.6. Mining is not new to the Hemerdon area. There are pits and old buildings and the photograph shows the modern china clay quarries, with huge white waste heaps standing on the skyline. These are the Lee Moor clay workings on the edge of Dartmoor National Park. The new tungsten processing plant would be in the valley. Most of the land in the centre of the photograph, Crownhill Down, would be covered by mine-waste. But the Down is popular with people from the nearby towns and villages, who use it for recreation.

Tungsten mining: another problem of prices and jobs

Hemerdon Ball is a granite hill on the edge of Dartmoor, 11 kilometres north east of Plymouth (see fig. 4.2). It contains **tungsten** ore, called wolframite. Britain spends about £16m to import tungsten each year, mainly from China, the USSR and North Korea. It is a **strategic metal** and a mine at Hemerdon Ball could supply most of Britain's needs for 20 years.

To develop the mine at Hemerdon Ball would cost about £50m and the mining company has spent over £7m in exploration and testing. The construction phase would involve 400 workers, with 350 permanent jobs once mining began. Most of these would be local, and other jobs might be created in the area by the **multiplier effect**, in total bringing roughly £12m to the local economy each year. The whole operation requires a huge open pit, processing plant, roads, service areas and disposal dumps to take 100m tonnes of waste rock over a 20 year period. Fig. 4.5 shows the extent of this operation.

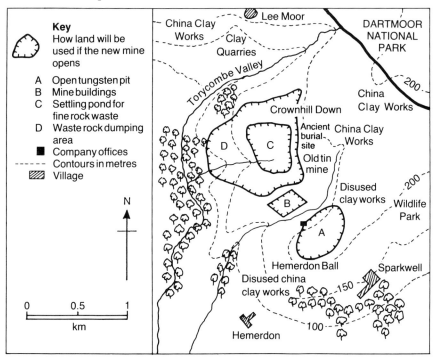

Key
How land will be used if the new mine opens
A Open tungsten pit
B Mine buildings
C Settling pond for fine rock waste
D Waste rock dumping area
■ Company offices
----- Contours in metres
▨ Village

To start mining, the company needed permission from the County Council. The Council has a policy for deciding whether to accept or refuse an application. This involves trying to weigh up the advantages against the disadvantages.

Use the labels in fig. 4.7 and make lists of the points you would put on either side of the balance.
What are the points for which it would be very difficult to measure the importance? For example, is the visual quality or attractiveness of the landscape easy to measure? Underline all these points in your lists.
Which things are most important in each list? Do you think the need for jobs is a major factor? Or the effect on those local inhabitants who will not get any economic benefits? Or the archaeological remains?

By now you should have an idea about which groups of people would be keen on the idea of the new mine and who might object. Make lists of these two groups.

There is much more information you would need to have before you could make a reasoned and careful judgement about the arguments for and against this new mine proposal. But how do you think you might have decided the result of this planning application? What are your reasons?

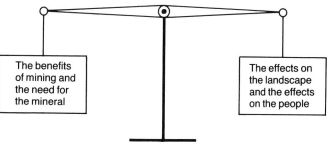

| The benefits of mining and the need for the mineral | The effects on the landscape and the effects on the people |

Fig. 4.7. Weighing up the arguments.

When the first application for the Hemerdon mine was made, the Secretary of State for the Environment ordered that there should be a **Public Inquiry**. The result of this Inquiry was that the mining application was refused, because the waste dump would alter the shape of Crownhill Down too much and destroy an old wood. The processing plant would be visually very obvious also. The mining company made changes to meet these objections to its plans and submitted a new application. This was accepted by Devon County Council in 1985. But by 1988 the construction of the mine had not begun. Why? The answer is to be found in fig. 4.8. The big fall in world demand and in the price of tungsten was made worse by the continued high production from Chinese mines, even when prices were very low. Having spent large sums in exploration and development, the owners of Hemerdon mine could not afford to go ahead with construction until the price increased.

The cycle shown in fig. 4.4 again fits the situation. But in West Cornwall, with its long tradition of mining and the few opportunities for alternative employment, the collapse in tin prices is seen as a disaster. On the other hand, 120 kilometres to the east, at Plympton, many of the local inhabitants regarded the fall in demand for tungsten with pleasure.

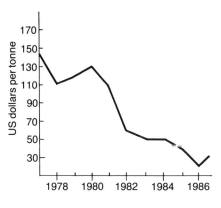

Fig. 4.8. World prices for tungsten concentrates.

Make a list of the differences in the two situations which might help to explain the different attitudes.

China clay: a problem of waste

Mining china clay or kaolin is the most important extractive industry in the South West and the English China Clay company is one of the biggest employers west of Bristol. The clay is found in several granite areas in Devon and Cornwall (fig. 4.2) where the rock has been changed chemically to produce funnel-shaped deposits. These can be mined by open-pit methods. The industry has several advantages:

(a) high quality deposits;
(b) good mining conditions;
(c) large reserves, enough for over 100 years;
(d) a large demand, both in Britain and abroad;
(e) closeness to the ports of Par, Fowey and Plymouth;
(f) a large-scale organisation, with one company controlling most of the clay deposits. It is the world's largest single producer of china clay and directly employs 5,000 people in Cornwall, and another 7,500 indirectly or in part-time jobs. (See fig. 7.22.)

With a high quality product for which there is a large market the industry has continued to expand its operations. It has one major problem. Each tonne of clay also produces about 8 tonnes of waste material: the overburden and broken granite, called stent, which are removed by mechanical diggers; and the mica which is washed out by the water-jets and settles in tanks. The result of these operations is shown in fig. 4.9.

Fig. 4.9. China clay workings and waste heaps on St Austell Moor. The mining company, English China Clays, describes the problem like this:

'For more than 200 years, these waste products have been tipped on land surrounding the opencast workings in huge dumps, some containing the overburden and stent, others of sand heaped up into great white pyramids, creating a unique and spectacular "lunar landscape" in an area of more than 50 square kilometres of mid-Cornwall. This is the legacy of intense industrial activity bringing with it inevitable environmental conflict'.

The danger of landslips on the spoil heaps, the local streams and coastline turned white with mica waste, and the prospect of the lunar landscape continually increasing in area, caused the mining company to begin a programme of reclamation in the 1970s. The high conical hills are being removed and waste is dumped in flatter heaps which are planted with grass or trees.

Fig. 4.10. China clay quarrying, waste disposal and reclamation. The model diagram shows the difference between old and new types of waste tip. It also explains why old pits are often not filled with waste. Underneath there may be reserves of clay which the mining company will want to get out in the future.

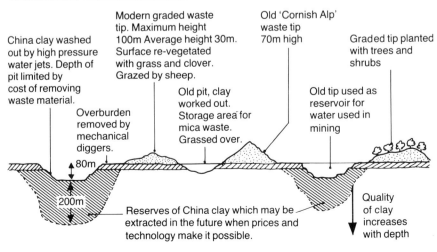

China clay washed out by high pressure water jets. Depth of pit limited by cost of removing waste material.

Modern graded waste tip. Maximum height 100m Average height 30m. Surface re-vegetated with grass and clover. Grazed by sheep.

Old 'Cornish Alp' waste tip 70m high

Graded tip planted with trees and shrubs

Overburden removed by mechanical diggers.

Old pit, clay worked out. Storage area for mica waste. Grassed over.

Old tip used as reservoir for water used in mining

80m

200m

Reserves of China clay which may be extracted in the future when prices and technology make it possible.

Quality of clay increases with depth

environmental impact

Most human activity has a direct effect on the physical environment. Waste products from factories, homes or farms get into the air, rivers or the sea. Noise can be disturbing for wildlife as well as other people. When vegetation is removed, rivers dammed to form lakes, minerals dug up or roads built, then the visual appearance of a place is changed. This visual effect is often the most obvious part of the total impact on the environment.

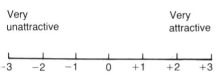

Fig. 4.11. Measuring the visual impact.

The effects of present mining operations, adding continually to the results of 200 years of quarrying, mean that there is an enormous task of reclamation. Some people think more money should be spent on improving the appearance of the devastated areas. The company argues that to extend the reclamation scheme to tackle all the derelict areas would be very expensive; this would then raise the price of Cornish china clay and make it less competitive against foreign producers. Probably the lunar landscape around St Austell will continue to be used as a location for making science fiction films. Its appearance provides a measure of the **environmental impact** which an activity like open-pit quarrying can have. A similar problem, though over a smaller area, occurs on the edge of the Dartmoor National Park at Lee Moor (fig. 4.6).

Compare the two photographs, fig. 4.9 and fig. 5.3(b). Use the scale (fig. 4.11) to make a judgement about the degree of visual impact which human activities have had in both the scenes.
Both landscapes have in fact been greatly affected and changed by human action. Perhaps in fig. 5.3(b) the changes are not so obvious and certainly not so unattractive. What kinds of landscape would you expect to put at the right-hand side of the scale?
Do you think that making judgements about visual impact is accurate and reliable? In your opinion does human activity always spoil the landscape? Discuss this method of measurement with a partner. How do your opinions compare on the landscapes shown in other photographs? (You might find figs. 3.2 and 5.7 useful in doing this.)
Can you suggest improvements to this method of measuring visual impact?

In the past mining often caused serious environmental damage without causing great public protest. Today the essential argument at St Austell, Hemerdon and elsewhere is between economic benefit and environmental costs.

Rock for building

Out of the 10 British regions the South West is the largest producer of limestone, third in the production of igneous rock and fifth for sand and gravel output. These construction **aggregates** far exceed metal ores and china clay in value (see Table 10) and they are an important source of local employment.

Using fig. 4.2 find and name the areas most important for the quarrying of limestone, granite and basic igneous rock.

aggregates

Concrete, roadstone, landfill and ballast all need broken rock which is produced by crushing to various sizes. Gravel occurs naturally in convenient sizes.

Fig. 4.12. Batts Combe quarry on the edge of the Mendip Hills near Cheddar Gorge. This limestone quarry produces 1.4 million tonnes of rock annually. It is used for roadstone, lime, and by the steel industry in South Wales. About 100 people are employed at this quarry.

Wytch Farm and the oil industry

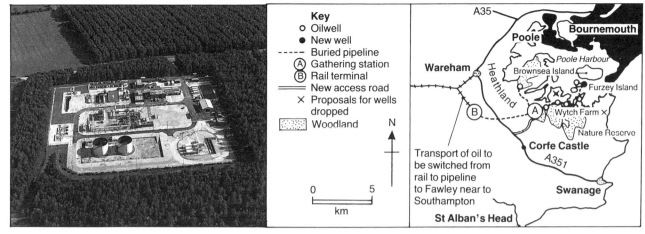

Fig. 4.13. The gathering station at Wytch Farm oilfield. This is the collection point for the oil from the production wells.

Fig. 4.14. Location of the BP oilfield on the Isle of Purbeck.

Area of Outstanding Natural Beauty (AONB)

Areas with attractive scenery where the natural beauty is worth protecting for both local and national interests. The use of these areas is restricted to conserve the landscape.

In 1974 Britain's largest onshore oilfield was discovered in the area known as the Isle of Purbeck in Dorset. It is an **Area of Outstanding Natural Beauty** and some people feared that the drilling and production installations would intrude upon the landscape and seriously disturb wildlife. Despite opposition from conservationists, the oilfield was exploited because, although much smaller than most of the North Sea fields, the production costs are much lower. In order to tap deeper oil reserves and increase production the oil company, BP, applied to Dorset County Council in 1986 for permission to expand its operations in the Wytch Farm area. The arguments used were of two main kinds:

(a) Economic: £46m would be spent with local construction and engineering firms and other suppliers of goods and services; up to 1,400 jobs would be created during construction; about 400 permanent jobs would be available during the 20 year life of the oilfield.

(b) Environmental: there would be no new large-scale changes to the landscape as most of the expansion would take place on existing sites and extra pipelines and storage tanks would be buried; the development of the oilfield up to 1986 showed that the company was very concerned to minimise the environmental impact.

Use the photograph (fig. 4.13) and the map (fig. 4.14) to identify steps taken by BP to lessen the visual impact of oil extraction.
After public discussions a number of changes were made to the plans for expansion. These included a reduction in the number of wells and pipelines, and a switch from rail to pipeline for the transport of oil to the refinery. These changes are shown on the map (fig. 4.14).
Can you think of any arguments which might have been made in favour of these changes?

The expansion at Wytch Farm depended on the building of a pipeline to the oil terminal on Southampton Water, a distance of 75km. Permission to construct it was given in 1987, its route taking it along the edge of the New Forest.

---

permeable rock

This is rock which will allow water to pass through it. There are two main reasons for this:
(i) the rock has spaces or pores between the mineral particles from which it is formed.
(ii) the rock has joints or cracks running through it.

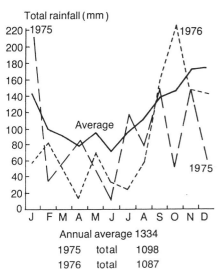

Fig. 4.15. Rainfall variations in Devon. 1975 and 1976 were drier than average. Summer drought in 1976 caused reservoirs to dry up, with water rationing in many areas. Reservoirs filled again with the heavy rainfall in the autumn.

Total rainfall (mm)

Annual average 1334

1975	total	1098
1976	total	1087

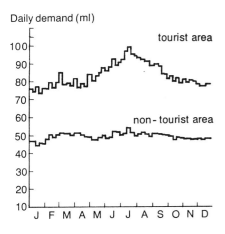

Fig. 4.16. Effect of holiday visitors on water demand Devon.

Table 13 *Comparative costs of reservoir construction.*

Roadford	£26 m
Bickleigh	£29 m
Swincombe	£27 m

Meeting the need for water

There are two ways of obtaining water for domestic and industrial consumption. Firstly there are surface supplies from rivers, lakes and artificial reservoirs; and secondly there are underground sources found in very **permeable** rocks called aquifers. These can be tapped by wells and boreholes. South West Water obtains about 13% of its supplies from groundwater but Wessex Water, which has much larger aquifers, gets 45%.

One important aquifer (labelled C on fig. 4.2) is formed by sandstones and breccias formed in Permian and Triassic times. Use fig. 3.1 to find out which rocks form the other three aquifers (A, B, D).
Fig. 4.2 shows the location of major reservoirs. Why are there no reservoirs inside the boundaries of the aquifers? Is there any pattern to the location of reservoirs in Devon?

In areas which are very dependent on surface sources such as rivers, a major problem can be caused by variations in rainfall input. Long droughts can also affect supplies from lakes and reservoirs. Reservoirs are, however, the obvious way of overcoming the problems of rainfall fluctuations. The storage of water is also necessary because demand varies. Short-term variations over a day or a week usually show a regular pattern and are not large enough to cause problems. Seasonal changes can be more difficult to manage; one example is the increase in demand which results from the influx of summer visitors into parts of the South West, as fig. 4.16 shows.

There are other reasons why water-consumption may grow, for example, increases in the permanent resident population and improvements in living standards. These trends are studied by the water authorities and future demands are carefully forecast. Since the 1960s there has been a need to improve the water supplies to both North Devon and Plymouth, as fig. 4.17 shows. There are no large aquifers to provide an answer and new supplies must come from rivers or reservoirs.

Reservoirs had to be the answer to the problem described above. But this prompts other questions such as 'How many reservoirs? Which are the best locations?'. South West Water investigated over 100 possible sites and decided that physical conditions were suitable at several places. One of these, Swincombe, is in the Dartmoor National Park and had been rejected as a possible reservoir in 1970. Another, in a deep, wooded valley near Plymouth, had caused protests from many people when it was proposed in 1974. The drought years of 1975 and 1976 now made the problem an urgent one and SWW looked again at possible solutions, working out the building costs of each. Table 13 shows a third site, at Roadford, to be the cheapest.

What were the other factors which made it the first choice? They included:

(a) Hydrology: the River Wolf provides a reliable water supply. The location fits into the existing system for distributing water.

(b) Geology and relief: the valley has a suitable shape and has a storage capacity large enough to meet needs until the year 2001 at least. The rock foundations are watertight and unlikely to be affected by earthquakes.

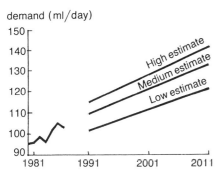

Fig. 4.17. Expected demand for water in Plymouth in the future.

Fig. 4.18. Valley of the River Wolf. The base of the dam is being built between the two woods. The dam will be 445 m long, 39 m high and will flood an area of 295 hectares.

(c) Social and economic aspects: most of the farmland which will be flooded is not high quality and is used for cattle pasture or rough grazing.

The population in the valley is small and is scattered in farms and hamlets.

There are no rare or important communities of plants and wild animals or any valuable archaeological remains.

There are no large centres of population downstream from the reservoir which would be in danger if the dam broke.

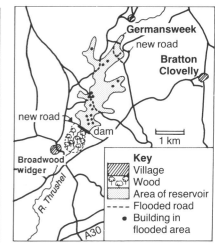

Fig. 4.19. Site of Roadford Reservoir.

Although the water authority built up a good argument for Roadford some people argued the opposite, pointing out the disadvantages:

1. 300 hectares of land would be flooded and another 470 hectares affected because farms would be split up or reduced in size. Over one third of this farmland was of Grade 3 (average) quality and therefore too valuable to be lost to food production.
2. Thirteen farms would become uneconomic or difficult to manage and two jobs would be lost.
3. There is little chance of other employment in the area if jobs are lost. Families have to move elsewhere, damaging the social life of small communities.
4. The reservoir would attract sightseers and the local roads could not cope with the extra traffic.
5. Five old buildings would be destroyed.
6. The Wolf valley is traditional English landscape, unspoilt by main roads, railways or electricity pylons. This landscape and the natural habitat of wildlife would be damaged by the reservoir, visitors and traffic.

'Don't use this valley because it will damage farming and rural life. Use Swincombe or another site on Dartmoor where people and agricultural land will not be directly affected.'

What might the following people think about this statement:
(a) an old person who has always lived in the Roadford area?
(b) a holiday-maker who visits Dartmoor every year to enjoy the scenery?
(c) an hotel-owner in North Devon?

Swincombe wanted as S.W. reservoir

SAVE FARM LAND URGES DEVON M.P.

THE PRESERVATION of good agricultural land was urged in the Commons yesterday by Mr. Peter Mills, M.P. for West Devon.

Proposals for a large reservoir and dam in the Roadford Valley, Devon, the biggest project of its kind ever planned for the South-west, will meet strong opposition from the Ministry of Agriculture and the National Farmers' Union.

Farmers line up against £30M Devon reservoir proposal

Fig. 4.20. Reservoirs in the news.

5 Farming

Farming is a very important activity in the South West and creates much of the wealth of the region. The type of farming varies from one place to another because it is linked to differences in the quality of the land. This affects the kinds of crops which can be grown and the productivity of the land. Fig. 5.1 shows the main differences in land quality.

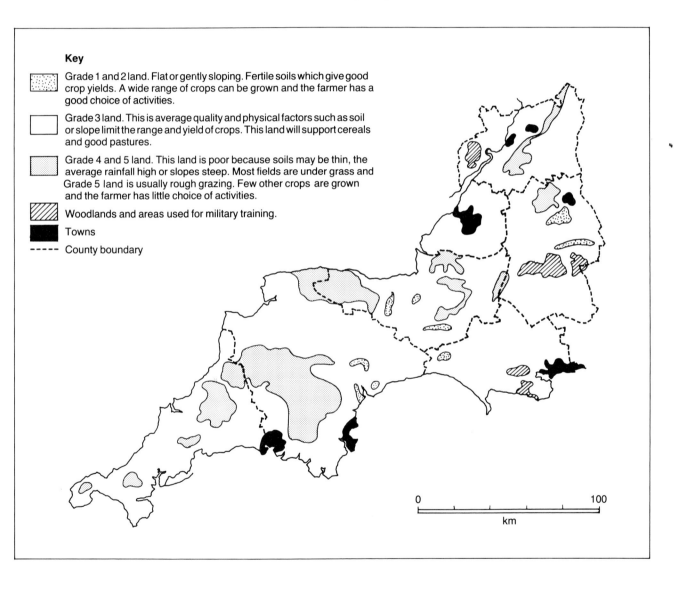

Key

Grade 1 and 2 land. Flat or gently sloping. Fertile soils which give good crop yields. A wide range of crops can be grown and the farmer has a good choice of activities.

Grade 3 land. This is average quality and physical factors such as soil or slope limit the range and yield of crops. This land will support cereals and good pastures.

Grade 4 and 5 land. This land is poor because soils may be thin, the average rainfall high or slopes steep. Most fields are under grass and Grade 5 land is usually rough grazing. Few other crops are grown and the farmer has little choice of activities.

Woodlands and areas used for military training.

Towns

- - - - County boundary

0   100
km

Fig. 5.1. Quality of farmland.

We can use this map to investigate some of the connections between physical factors and the quality of farmland. Find maps of relief and rainfall in an atlas. Which areas of poorer grade 4 and 5 land in the South West match up with areas of higher ground and higher rainfall? List the names of these upland areas.

43

You should have noticed (fig. 5.1) that there are only small areas of the best quality (Grades 1 and 2) land in the region. Farmers in these areas are able to grow a wide range of crops and therefore have a big choice in the kind of farming they carry out. Most farmers have average, Grade 3, land to work with and so they must make an extra effort to maintain the fertility and productivity of their farms.

Fig. 5.2. Factors which affect decisions on the farm. There are several, in addition to physical ones, over which the individual farmer has little control.

Farmer has little control			Farmer has most control		Farmer has little control	
1	2	3	4	5	6	7
Physical factors	Farm size	Equipment and building	Knowledge and skills	Production costs	Market prices	Government cash and support

Personal knowledge or skill are things a farmer can influence and it is important that a farmer keeps up-to-date with modern methods. At the same time a farmer can try to influence the way other factors, shown in fig. 5.2, affect the management of the farm.

Livestock farming on Dartmoor

Fig. 5.3. Much of the farm is on higher land, over 300 m above sea-level. Inside the wall the field has been improved for permanent grass pasture. Beyond the wall is heather moorland which is also used for rough grazing. The farmer's grazing rights extend beyond the tor on the skyline.

This farm lies on the edge of the granite upland of Dartmoor. The way the land is used is shown in fig. 5.4.

Most of the land is poor quality, Grade 5, and there is a very limited choice in the type of farming possible. In the twelve years from 1975 to 1987 the farmer made a number of decisions which affected the economy of the farm and its productivity.

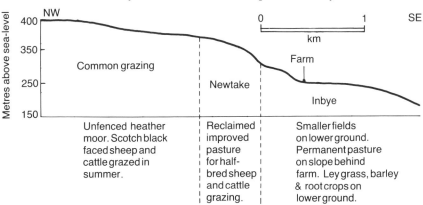

Fig. 5.4. Cross-section showing land use on the farm.

Table 14 *Major changes on a Dartmoor farm.*

1975	1987	Reasons
73 ha of cropland	89 ha of cropland	Better quality land bought from neighbour to increase winter fodder crops of barley, silage grass, beet and swedes for cattle and sheep.
4.5 ha of rough grazing improved	Another 7 ha of grazing improved	By improving the quality of the pasture the farmer can keep more stock and increase his productivity. But there will be no more reclamation of this kind. The farmer agreed with the Dartmoor National Park Authority to leave some boulders and rough vegetation in the newly reclaimed area. Another agreement with the National Park will leave the higher ground in its present state and the farmer will receive payments to offset the loss of income.
450 Scotch black-face ewes. Lambs sold in Exeter to local farmers for fattening	450 Scotch black-face ewes. Lambs taken by lorry to West Midlands	The dry summer of 1976 forced Devon farmers to find grazing for their stock outside the region. The link with the West Midlands has continued. 140 lambs are taken by lorry and bring a better profit than at Exeter market.
200 half-bred ewes, lambs sold in Exeter for fattening by local farmers	300 half-bred ewes, most lambs are now finished on the farm and sold direct to the meat trade	The carrying-capacity of the farm has been improved by (a) the purchase of more fields from which more fodder crops are grown. (b) rough grazing turned into better grassland. (c) all pastures improved by use of more fertilizers. Better quality feeding means lambs can be sold direct to the meat trade because people now prefer lean meat and the lambs do not need fattening on lowland pastures. The farmer gets better prices.
100 cross-bred cattle	140 cross-bred cattle	The herd has increased because of increased fodder production. Another change is the use of Charollais bulls for breeding. This produces a larger, more valuable calf for fattening. The young stock are sold to lowland farmers.

less-favoured areas

These are areas where the land is infertile and productivity is below the national average. It is part of the agricultural policy of the European Community to help farmers in these areas with cash subsidies. In the South West this classification applies to Exmoor, Dartmoor and the granite moors of Cornwall. They are called areas of **marginal farming**.

Fig. 5.5. Cash support available to the Dartmoor farmer.

Copy out the list of factors in fig. 5.2 and use the information in Table 14 to show what decisions have been made on the way this farm is run.

One very important factor for farmers in areas like Dartmoor is the help given by the European Community and the British Government. This farm qualifies for grants of money because it is in a **less-favoured area**. The land is mainly suitable for livestock production and crops are grown only to feed the farm animals. Extra money is paid for cows and ewes which are kept for breeding. This helps to make up for the low productivity and to raise the farmer's income. It encourages hill-farmers to stay in these less-favoured areas and to conserve the appearance of the countryside. So hill-farms like this one on Dartmoor may have two extra sources of income (fig. 5.5).

Copy the diagram (fig. 5.5) and against each of the two arrows write down the reasons for these payments. What would happen if the European Community stopped its payments? Would the farmer still be willing to agree to the restrictions suggested by the National Park Authority? How might the appearance of the landscape change in areas of hill-farming?

In 1987 the British government offered farmers in **marginal areas** a payment to reduce the production of cereal crops. Farmers must agree to leave fallow at least 20% of their cereal area and to plant trees on it or use it for non-agricultural projects like caravan parks or golf courses.

If the Dartmoor hill-farmer accepted this agreement how would it affect the running of the farm? How might this proposal conflict with the policy of the National Park?

A cereal and sheep farm on Salisbury Plain

This is a very large farm near Stonehenge and has been formed by joining up several smaller farms which are now run as one unit. It specialises in the production of cash crops and is run by a board of directors with a manager to give advice and carry out decisions. Fig. 5.6 shows the main features of the farm economy.

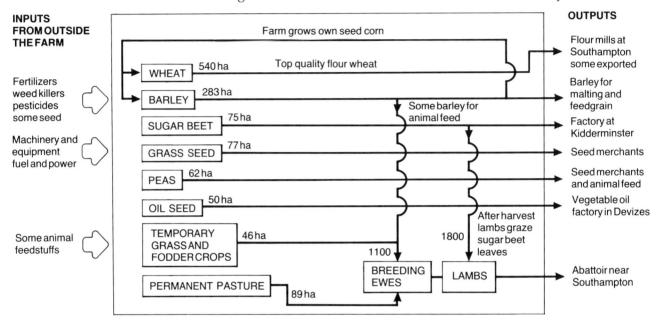

Fig. 5.6. Types of crops, livestock, outputs and markets.

Use the information in the diagram to write a short description of the economy of the farm. Draw bar-graphs to show the area used for each crop.

The farm is Grade 3 quality land. There are some areas which are difficult to farm, because the slopes are steep or the ground is wet in the valley bottoms, but the main handicap is that the soil is not of high fertility. To maintain good yields the manager keeps a regular rotation of crops and uses large amounts of fertilizer. In this way there can be a large choice of crops to grow. Since the manager's main concern is to keep up the profits for the owners, the manager must judge which products will fetch the highest prices. Also, production costs must be watched carefully. These are some of the decisions made in recent years:

(i) Cut the size of the flock of breeding ewes from 3,000 to 1,100. This was done because lamb prices had become less attractive.

(ii) Delay the sale of lambs from autumn until winter, when prices are higher.

(iii) Grow peas, now that new varieties make harvesting easier.

(iv) Reduce the labour force by two tractor-drivers and one shepherd. In addition to the manager there are 12 people employed full-time on the farm. At busy times, for example for sheep-shearing, a team of **contract labour** is hired for a few days.

Draw a copy of fig. 5.2 and use it to record the information about the management of this cereal and sheep farm.

Because there is an over-production of most crops and animal products in the countries of the European Community, the British government is advising farmers to find other ways of using their land. At present this farm concentrates on high quality products

contract labour

Some tasks on a farm need extra labour. The farmer may hire a team of workers who travel from farm to farm to do a particular job. Some tasks need expensive equipment too, and the farmer will hire this as well. A good example is harvesting.

Table 15 *Surplus stocks of food held in store by the European Community in June, 1988 (in thousands of tonnes).*

Butter	439
Skim Milk	109
Beef	760
Wheat	6110
Barley	3700

Fig. 5.7. Cereal and sheep farm on Salisbury Plain. Compare this photograph with the Dartmoor farm (fig. 5.3).

which bring the top price. One possible choice is to change to organic farming, since organic produce at present brings higher prices. This would mean stopping the use of artificial fertilizers, chemical weedkillers and pesticides. The control of weeds would become a problem and could cause difficulties in the production of high quality grass seed and other high value crops. The farm manager has therefore decided that this would not be a good solution. Instead the manager expects to increase the recreational use of the farm by:
(a) using some of the old farm cottages for holiday accommodation in summer;
(b) renovating stables on the farm to develop a riding school;
(c) charging visitors who take part in game-shoots on the farm.

A dairy farm in Somerset

This is a small, intensive farm which specialises in milk production with a herd of 80 pedigree Friesian cows. Because of the pedigree the heifer calves bring a good price when sold to other farmers, although some are kept for replacements in the farm's milking herd. The layout and position of the farm cause two problems:

(i) It is split up into four blocks which makes management difficult. The farmhouse and the main block of fields are on a low ridge. The dairy herd cannot be grazed on the other blocks because it would take too long to bring them to the milking parlour each day. These distant fields are used for silage and hay and also to graze heifers which do not produce milk.

(ii) The lowest land floods each winter and cannot be cultivated. It is therefore under permanent pasture. The slopes of the ridge are too steep for ploughing and are also in permanent pasture, as fig. 5.8 shows. The temporary grassland on the higher fields needs a good supply of rain to stimulate grass growth. In dry summers such as 1987 the poor pastures force the farmer to give manufactured feedstuff to the cows to maintain milk yields. But this greatly increases the production costs.

47

Fig. 5.8. Dairy farm in Somerset. The flat land and the sloping sides of the ridge are used for permanent pasture. The lowland is part of the area called the Somerset Levels.

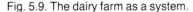

HUMAN INPUTS
include:

1 Farmer's decisions
2 3 full- time workers
3 Manufactured cattle feed
4 Artificial fertilizers
5 Fuel for machinery
6 Local straw for bedding

NATURAL INPUTS
include:

1 The weather mild and moist (average rainfall 640 mm annually)
2 Flooding of lower pastures in winter

FARM STRUCTURAL FEATURES

1 50 hectares in 4 blocks
2 Buildings for milking, housing cattle in winter and storage
3 16 hectares of rented pasture
4 Land slopes from ridge to low drained fields
5 Soils give good pastures in average weather conditions
6 Milking machines
  3 tractors
  1 ditcher
  1 hay baler
  1 tillage machine

FARM ACTIVITIES

1 80 cows grazed on summer pasture Stall-fed in winter
2 75 heifers grazed and stall-fed
3 Pastures ploughed and re-sown every 2 or 3 years
4 Turnips or kale sown for winter fodder
5 Silage and hay cut by contractors
6 Irrigation of pastures in dry summers
7 Grass fertilized in spring and summer
8 Cattle milked twice each day

OUTPUTS

Milk sold to creamery at Wellington

Heifer calves sold

Bull calves sold for meat

Fig. 5.9. The dairy farm as a system.

Table 16 *Annual Milk Quota for a Somerset farm (in litres).*

1983	411,165
1984	451,165
1985	451,165
1986	426,124
1987	400,108

Study fig. 5.9 and make lists of:
(a) the main production costs on the farm;
(b) the ways in which the farmer tries to increase production and farm income;
(c) examples of the influence of physical factors on the management of the farm.

Most of the income comes from milk production and the farm is organised for this purpose. In 1982, to intensify the use of the farm and to increase the income, the farmer spent £20,000 on a new milking parlour. A larger herd of 100 cows could then be kept, raising the milk output.

But because many farmers had steadily improved their outputs there was a large surplus of milk in the European Community. To reduce this surplus, restrictions on production for the Community's member states were announced in 1983. In Britain each farmer is given an annual quota. Milk produced above the quota receives a lower payment. Table 16 shows the annual quota for this dairy farm in Somerset. In 1984 the farmer bought a quota of 40,000 litres from a neighbour, whose small dairy herd had been sold, and rented the grazing land.

Table 17 *Use of concentrated cattle feed: milk yield (per cow).*

	Feed (kg)	Yield (litres)
1983	1300	6000
1987	650	5400

Fig. 5.10. The Somerset Levels. Drainage ditches carry water to larger dykes, from which it is pumped into rivers. Farmers can improve the land quality and grow more profitable crops by installing better pumps. But this changes the habitat for wildlife like the otter, and for birds which feed on the wet land in winter and nest here in summer. In the areas most important for wildlife protection, farmers are now being paid for not changing the methods of drainage.

Environmentally Sensitive Area

A geographical area with special qualities of scenery, wildlife or archaeology which could easily be destroyed by human action. In an ESA the farmers are paid to use methods of farming which benefit the environment.

The farm's quota was reduced by almost 10% from 1985 to 1987, which is equal to the yield from ten cows. The penalties for over-production have been increased. What should the farmer do?

(a) Reduce the size of the herd?
(b) Change from dairy farming to growing cereals or raising beef?
(c) Reduce the milk yield of each cow and cut costs of production?

The farmer chose the third solution, using smaller amounts of a cheaper concentrated feed. Table 17 shows the effect on the average milk yield per cow. This decision is not surprising, because:

(a) the land is suited to grass production;
(b) years had been spent building up a pedigree herd;
(c) all the specialist equipment needed for dairy farming had already been bought;
(d) the farmer knows a lot about running a dairy herd.

But now, because there is the problem of over-production, the farmer cannot rely upon milk as the main source of income. The farm cannot be made much more efficient and so a financial adviser was asked to suggest other ways in which the farmer could earn money. The advice gave several possibilities:

1. set up a caravan camping site.
2. make the farm into a golf-course.
3. open a farm shop. (Some butter and cream is already sold at the farmhouse, but there would be a need to grow vegetables too.)
4. rent the land for riding, shooting and fishing.
5. open the farm to tourists and set up a tea-shop.
6. convert part of the building into a restaurant.
7. convert part of the farmhouse to holiday accommodation and let it to summer visitors.

Analyse these seven choices under lists with these headings:
(a) would cause most change to the present land use;
(b) would need new knowledge and skill by the farmer;
(c) would be easy to fit into the present pattern of land use and farm management.
After studying the choices which do you think is the most practicable? How would it affect the farm as a system (fig. 5.9)?

The farmer has decided that the last choice is the most attractive and so part of the farmhouse will be used for holiday guests. The other choices will cost too much money and the investment will be too risky.

There is one other way in which the farmer could find additional sources of income. One third of the farm lies on low flat land called the Somerset Levels which are shown on fig. 3.33. This land was once marsh, but most of it has been drained artificially for pasture and cropland. Much of the Levels still floods in winter, however, which encourages a rich plant life in some places. There are important habitats for wild flowers, wading birds and rare animals like the otter.

In 1987 a large part of the Somerset Levels, totalling 27,000 hectares, was classed by the Government as an **Environmentally Sensitive Area**. Within this area farmers were invited to accept

Fig. 5.11. The thirteen Environmentally Sensitive Areas which were proposed in 1986.

restrictions on their farming methods in order to protect the environment; These restrictions are at two Tiers:

Tier one: the farmer agrees:
(a) to use less than 350 kg of fertilizer per hectare;
(b) not to plough;
(c) not to make improvements to drainage;
(d) to restrict the use of weedkillers;
(e) not to stock the fields heavily with animals;
(f) not to cut grass after 31st August each year;
By accepting these conditions the farmer would receive £82 per hectare of land affected.

Tier two: the farmer accepts all the tier one rules and agrees also:
(a) to use less than 175 kg of fertilizer per hectare;
(b) not to roll his fields between March and May;
(c) not to cut grass before the end of June;
(d) not to graze sheep after 31st October.
For these extra restrictions the farmer would receive £120 per hectare.

How will these restrictions help to protect the natural vegetation and wildlife? Suggest reasons for each of the rules in Tier one and Tier two.

Not all the farmers within the Environmentally Sensitive Area have accepted these agreements, which are voluntary. The dairy farmer, part of whose land lies within the Levels, has not yet decided. If he agrees then this will greatly reduce the **carrying capacity** of the farm. The low-lying fields could not be used for the intensive production of silage crops and the quality of the pastures would be reduced.

Patterns and changes in farming

The studies of the dairy farm in Somerset and of the other two farms have given you information about the factors shown in fig. 5.2.

Look again at this diagram.
What examples do you now have of the ways in which a farmer's decisions are influenced?
What do you think are the most difficult decisions that a farmer has to make about the management of the land?

Your answer to the last question might include the problem which some farmers had to face in 1987 and 1988. Should they completely alter the way their land is used? The British government is trying to persuade farmers to diversify, that is to increase the range of commercial activities and to use land for non-agricultural purposes. These new developments are part of the sequence of changes which have occurred in farming in the last 40 years. One of these changes is a reduction in the number of people employed in agriculture. Another is the increased yields from crops and animals (Tables 18 and 19).

Each hectare has more put into it in terms of energy, cultivation and chemical application so that it produces more cereals, more grass, more meat or more milk than before. Table 15 suggests that the same increases have happened in other European countries too.

carrying capacity
The farmer has 66 hectares of land to grow food for 155 cows and heifers. If the area of grass pasture is reduced or if less grass is cropped for silage, the main winter feed for the animals, then the capacity of the farm to support the herd is reduced also.

Table 18 *Full-time employment in agriculture in England and Wales.*

1970	1985
217,591	164,052

Table 19 *Changes in average yields in UK (tonnes per hectare).*

	1970	1985
Wheat	4.27	6.35
Barley	3.25	4.95

Remember that the effects are not always directly obvious. For example, it was once common farming practice to give fields a rest from continuous cropping by leaving them fallow. This also helped to clean the land of crop diseases and pests. Now crop yields can be maintained by the heavy use of fertilizers, and diseases can be tackled by treating with other chemicals.

These changes have affected the environment in the countryside in many ways, but they have not completely changed the types of farming to be found in the South West. Relief, soils and climate still influence the broad pattern of land use which is shown in fig. 5.12. By comparing this map with fig. 5.1 you can see this influence, particularly in the use of land of Grade 4 and 5 quality.

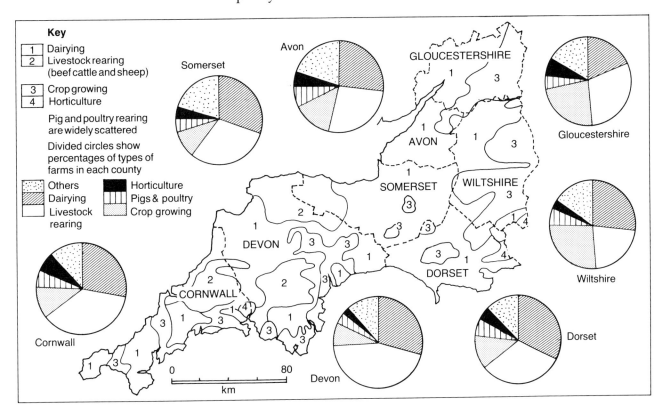

Fig. 5.12. Types of farming.

Use this generalised map of types of farming to build up a description of agriculture in the region. Begin by copying out the following sentences and then add your own sentences to complete the description for the whole of the South West:

Much of the land in the South West Region is used for dairy farming, especially in Dorset, Somerset and the central area of Devon. The main crop-growing areas are in the east and north of the region in Wiltshire and Gloucestershire.

Even though this chapter has been mainly about changes in farming, the description you have written will not go out-of-date. For a long time into the future the map will still show that a certain type of land use is important in a particular area. You can expect to see arable farms on Salisbury Plain or dairy farming in the plains and valleys in the future. But there are some recent changes which show that farmers are affected by the prices of their products and by restrictions which the Government and the European Community impose. In order to maintain their incomes some farmers will switch from one kind of farming and land use to another.

Table 20 *Changes in the use of farmland in three counties of the South West.*

Changes in main uses of farmland (in hectares)	Devon 1980	1985	Gloucestershire 1980	1985	Wiltshire 1980	1985
Cereals	72,000	73,200	76,900	81,300	110,800	114,500
Fodder crops	8,000	8,850	2,700	4,100	3,000	5,200
Temporary grass	80,400	79,000	27,600	25,300	41,300	39,000
Permanent grass	293,750	295,000	79,300	74,900	87,750	81,200
Changes in the numbers of types of farm						
Dairying	3,485	3,182	707	639	909	846
Lowland cattle and sheep	3,846	4,180	988	1,102	658	682
Cropping	903	849	686	763	741	808

The figures for the three counties show some of the changes in land use. Which of the following statements is supported by the figures in the Table? Between 1980 and 1985:

(a) the biggest change was in the area growing fodder crops;
(b) temporary grassland decreased in area;
(c) cereal cultivation became more important;
(d) permanent grassland decreased in area;
(e) the number of dairy farms decreased by about 10% in each county;
(f) the rearing of cattle and sheep on lowland farms became more important;
(g) there was an increase in the number of farms producing crops.

We can put some of these changes into a broader picture over a longer time period. In England and Wales the proportion of the land surface which is farmed altered little between 1947 (72.7% of the land area) and 1980 (71.8%). What changed was the way some of the land was used.

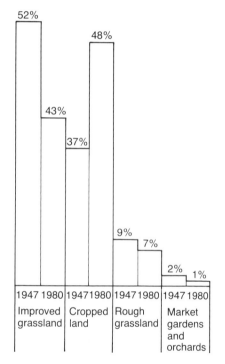

Fig. 5.13. Changes in the use of farmland in England and Wales.

Look at fig. 5.13. What are the main differences in the composition of farmland between those two dates?

6 The job scene

Of the South West's total population of just over 4 million, 1.5 million have jobs. This is one of the lowest proportions of employed people to total population for a region in the UK.

Four reasons helping to make this such a low proportion were mentioned in Chapter 2. What are they?

Making things

Look back at Table 8. You will see that just over one quarter of all those employed in the South West are in jobs in Employment Groups 2, 3 and 4. These are manufacturing and processing activities, and fig. 6.1 shows the logos of some of the firms engaged in these activities in South West England.

Write down one product made by each of these firms. Now place each product into one of the following groups:
(a) clothing and footwear;
(b) food and drink;
(c) engineering;
(d) other.

Home-made

The making of food and drink products in the South West is linked to the previous and present farming activities of the region. One output of the farms mentioned in Chapter 5 is fresh milk. This supplies the needs of people living in the region, but the total quantity of milk produced is greater than these needs. Some of the surplus (or remainder) is sent to the adjoining more densely populated regions of the South East and West Midlands. Many workers are engaged in this distribution by road and rail. Chapter 7 will show an additional market for fresh milk – the summer inflow of holiday visitors. Processing milk into butter, cheese, milk powder and yoghurt is yet another way of using the surplus. Throughout the South West, dairy factories (or creameries) employ many people in such activities, for example, at Milborne St Andrew in Dorset (Express Dairies) and Torrington in Devon (Unigate).

Fig. 6.1. The logos of some of the manufacturing and processing firms located in the South West.

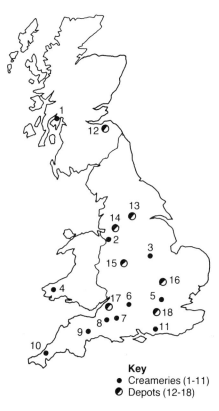

Key
- ● Creameries (1–11)
- ◐ Depots (12–18)

Fig. 6.2. The location in Great Britain of the 11 creameries and 7 depots belonging to St Ivel Ltd. (It is part of the Unigate group of companies.)

Is 'scattered' or 'clustered' the better word to use to describe this pattern of distribution? What benefit can the firm gain from having this distribution pattern?

Near Swindon, a creamery at Wootton Bassett (number 8 in fig. 6.2) started there in 1913. Since then, it has grown in size to occupy a 10.5 hectare site and provide 600 jobs. No longer are 17-gallon (78 litre) churns rolled from farm carts into the factory. Now, most milk from over 360 farms is collected by a fleet of 9,000 litre refrigeration road tankers. Once at the creamery, all handling, storage and movement of the milk is controlled by a micro-processor. Yoghurt is the main product, but cottage cheese and skimmed milk are also made. It is essential that distribution is done at strictly-controlled temperatures. 350 vehicles are used for this activity, supplying the seven depots shown in fig. 6.2 and hundreds of individual shops. Such distribution is another important type of employment in the South West.

Cheddar in Somerset is known world-wide as a centre for cheese-making. However, the original recipe for 'Cheddar cheese' is now copied by firms located in other parts of the United Kingdom and even overseas. For example, the largest factory in Europe making Cheddar cheese is in Devon, at North Tawton. Moreover, 'Irish Cheddar' and 'New Zealand Cheddar' are varieties now on sale at most supermarkets.

Meat products are another link with the region's farming background. Factories making meat pies, pâté or sausages are located at Taunton (Somerwest), Totnes (Harris) and Trowbridge (Bowyers). Cornwall is noted for its pasties. At Callington one factory alone employs 600 people to make them. The firm Ginsters uses 80 articulated lorries and vans to deliver daily to depots at Bristol, Birmingham, London and Winchester. From these depots, shops and public houses all over the southern half of England and Wales can be supplied.

On an outline map of England and Wales, mark in the location of the Ginster factory and depots. Using a motoring organisation's handbook, draw in a main route, and its total distance in kilometres, from the factory to each depot. Assuming an average speed of 60 kph, how long does it take lorry drivers to deliver pasties to each depot from Callington, have a two-hour break, and return to the factory? Do the driving regulations of the European Community allow these journeys to be completed in one day?

Fig. 6.3. Some meat and dairy products linked with the South West's farming activities.

Help from outside

In the eighteenth and nineteenth centuries, very wealthy woollen industries existed in the sheep-rearing areas of the Cotswold Hills, Dartmoor and the Wiltshire Downs. At the peak of its operations, Bradford-on-Avon in Wiltshire had thirty woollen mills and cloth workshops. Today, it has none. Only in a few towns, e.g. Stroud (Gloucestershire) and Tiverton (Devon), do textile industries remain. Not enough wool is now produced within the region, and firms rely upon imports from Australia and New Zealand. The original reason for being located in the South West has almost disappeared. Long experience and technical skill however, enable these firms to remain in the South West and compete against others located in what are now more favourable areas of the United Kingdom or overseas. **Industrial inertia** operates. Rather than mass-produce goods, the firms specialise in the type or quality of the goods they make. For example, in Devon, Axminster is famous for carpets, Buckfastleigh for blankets and Dartington for tweeds.

industrial inertia
Industry continues to operate where it began, even though the reasons for that location have ceased to be so important.

To many people, the name 'Clarks' is linked with shoes. Local farms provided the raw materials of sheepskins and cow-hides for a factory which started at Street (Somerset) in 1828. Today, most of the materials are imported. To meet the increasing demand for shoes and slippers, the firm set up factories at several other locations in the South West (fig. 6.4), and now employs over 6,000 people within the region.

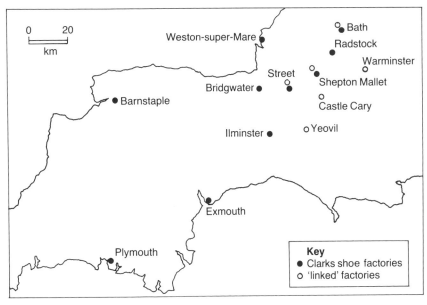

Fig. 6.4. Where Clarks have their shoe factories in the South West.

Why might Clarks have decided it was better to increase its output by having several factories throughout the region rather than by enlarging its existing factory at Street?

Street is the firm's headquarters, responsible for the organisation and distribution of goods across the United Kingdom to over 3,000 shops, many of which are owned by the firm itself. A firm such as Clarks has to alter its products frequently in order to keep up with changing fashion. This is especially true of ladies and teenage footwear.

industrial linkage
A trade connection where the flow of output from one firm becomes the input of another.

Special chemicals and techniques are needed by the shoe industry, e.g. for making polyurethane soles and for joining rubber soles to leather uppers. Specialist **linkage firms** exist for this at, for example, Shepton Mallet, Warminster and Yeovil (fig. 6.4), all within easy reach of the shoe factories.

Because it has had no large quantities of its own coal and metal ores, the South West has few areas producing heavy manufactured goods. Avonmouth (fig. 6.5) and Poole are exceptions, because the raw materials can be imported there. For example, lead and zinc are unloaded at Avonmouth, then moved by overhead conveyors to large blast furnaces where the ores are smelted.

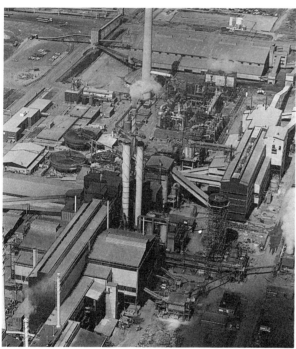

Fig. 6.5. Heavy industry located close to the docks at Avonmouth.

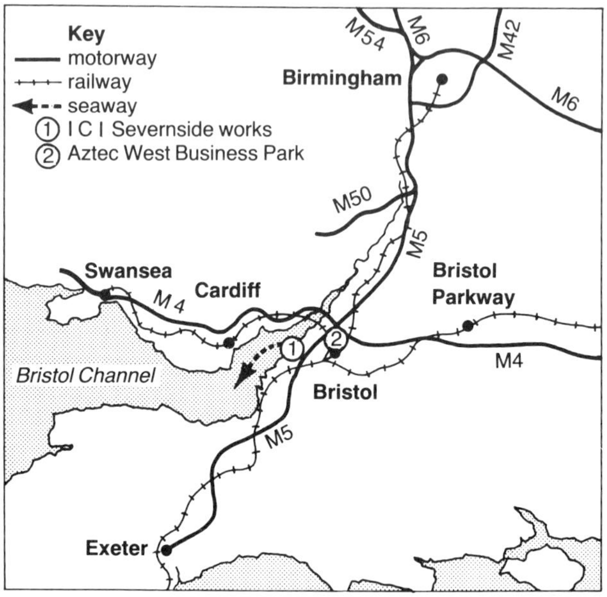

Fig. 6.6. The transport lines which allow the quick distribution of ICI's products.

Fertilizers and pharmaceuticals are also made at Avonmouth by Imperial Chemical Industries (ICI). In the making of these products:

(i) the phosphate rock is imported;
(ii) the rivers Avon and Severn provide the water required;
(iii) the estuary's strong tides remove and degrade the effluent;
(iv) power comes from the national grid (Chapter 8).

From fig. 6.6 you can see how easy it is for the Severnside works, which employ about 1,000 people, to distribute its products to southern England, Wales and the Midlands.

Flour-milling (Spillers) and chocolate-making (Cadbury-Schweppes) are other examples of activities in the region which were located where raw materials could be imported, for example at Bristol. The docks there were once the busiest in Britain, and processing factories grew up close to the docks. But the closure of the docks and the lack of space for expansion forced firms to find new locations, either in nearby towns, e.g. Keynsham, or at larger docks such as Avonmouth (fig. 8.8).

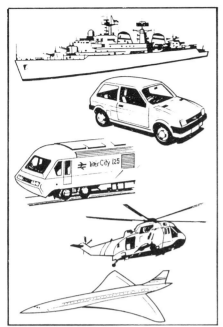

Fig. 6.7. Some engineering products linked with the South West.

Engineers everywhere

The products shown in fig. 6.7 have at least two features in common – each is a form of transport, and each is an output of an engineering industry which for a long time has been an important activity in the South West. Farming, tin-mining and clothing/footwear industries need machinery for their operations. Specialist engineering firms cater for their needs, for example at Hayle (West Cornwall), Lydney (NW Gloucestershire) and Melksham (Wiltshire).

However, engineering employment in some small and medium-sized towns is linked to the activities of just one or two firms. In Paignton (South Devon), 2,300 employees work in two factories within an area which lacks manufacturing jobs in general. This puts the town in a dangerous position if a firm cannot compete against others and has to reduce output or close down altogether. The loss of 500 jobs at the Comp-Air Holman factory at Camborne (West Cornwall) in 1985 was a severe blow to the town, which had no real alternative employment.

Filton (Avon) is the location of a Rolls-Royce factory which specialises in making aircraft engines. Adjoining it is British Aerospace, designing and manufacturing products for:
  (i) military aircraft (Nimrod, Tornado);
 (ii) guided weapons systems (Rapier, Seawolf);
(iii) civil aircraft (European Airbus, Skylark).

Keeping a position at the front of world technology needs a workforce with a wide range of advanced engineering skills. The company also requires much space – for present production, testing of products and future expansion. The area meets all of these needs. Over 11,000 people are employed at the British Aerospace factories at Filton, Plymouth and Weymouth.

Fig. 6.8. The Optica Scout spotter plane is a new idea. The specialist research, building and testing are carried out at a former airfield at Old Sarum.

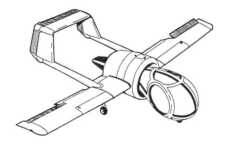

growth industry
In order to meet more demand, the industry expands at a rate which is faster than other sections of employment.

Westland, Britain's only maker of helicopters for civilian and military use, is located at Yeovil (Somerset). It has 10,000 employees. Like other parts of the engineering industry, it is a **growth industry**. It does, however, depend upon the decisions taken by the national government to increase or decrease the level of the country's defence programme.

The Royal Dockyard at Devonport (fig. 6.9) is also vulnerable to any decisions to alter the level of its activities, because it employs about 8,000 people and is therefore one of the largest employers in the whole of the Plymouth area.

Fig. 6.9. Devonport dockyard, now privately owned. It is a major base for the repairing and refitting of naval warships and nuclear submarines.

Estates for industry

The District of Thamesdown, which includes Swindon, has many **industrial estates**. Some of them are mapped in fig. 6.10. They were built to lower the area's dependence upon a single large activity. This was British Rail's engine and carriage workshops, first set up there by Brunel in 1841.

industrial estate
An area chosen by government (national or local) or a private company so that industrial activities can cluster in one location.

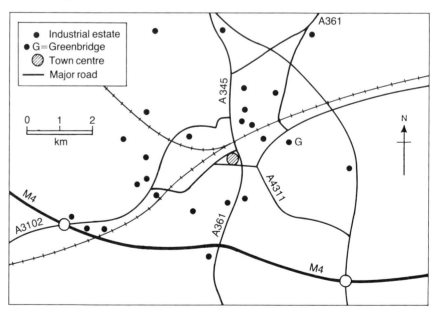

Fig. 6.10. The major industrial estates of Thamesdown.

What percentage of the Thamesdown estates is:
(a) less than 2 km from the town centre?
(b) less than 1 km from a major road?
For each of these locations, suggest two advantages and two disadvantages for a firm being located there.

One of these estates (G in fig. 6.10) is Greenbridge. 3,300 people are employed there, and below is a list of their activities:

making food products	making word processors
printing	making motor vehicle parts
book publishing	footwear manufacture
food distribution	making bathroom fittings
door manufacture	making children's clothing

Firms need space to make and store their products. They also require it for distribution lorries, employees' cars, possibly a canteen and even a sports' field. Such space is not available in the centre of towns. Because of this, firms have tended to locate near the outskirts of towns, where the cost of land is lower. However, their use of large amounts of land can lead to conflict with rural communities especially where the quality of farmland is high. A good deal of high grade land, of which there is only a small quantity in Devon (fig. 5.1) was lost to food production forever when an industrial estate (fig. 6.11) and a motorway interchange/services area were built on the outskirts of Exeter.

Fig. 6.11. Sowton Industrial Estate, Exeter, with the M5 motorway in the background. Most buildings are large and single-storey. Plenty of space has been left for delivery lorries, employees' cars, trees and gardens.

Fig. 6.12. Small workshop units at Lapford, Devon.

In rural areas, County Councils have worked in partnership with two national agencies (The Council for Small Industries in Rural Areas (CoSIRA) and English Estates) to build blocks of craft workshop units (fig. 6.12). Each unit employs from 1 to 10 workers, for example in the small villages of Mere (Somerset) and Tregony (Cornwall).

Fig. 6.13. A direction sign on the A38 dual carriageway approaching Plymouth. An estate at Langage is too new to be included.

Moving in

Many firms have been attracted into the South West from other regions of the UK. This is partly the result of plans by national government to encourage manufacturing away from urban and more congested areas. It has also increased the number of manufacturing jobs in places where there are few. All the **infrastructure** (roads, power and water supplies, etc.) is completed in advance, so that firms can move with the minimum of fuss. Firms have also been given grants to persuade them to move. In this way Plymouth has attracted firms from the South East and West Midlands on to its many industrial estates during the last 20 years (fig. 6.13). Some of these firms have moved *all* their operations from their original site, e.g. Wrigleys, who moved their chewing-gum factory from Wembley in 1971. Other firms have set up a branch of their operations in Plymouth while keeping their headquarters elsewhere, e.g. Plessey.

Firms from overseas have also been attracted into the South West – especially from Japan and the USA. For example, Becton Dickinson, the largest healthcare company in the USA, set up a branch factory in Plymouth in 1981, to produce sterile tubes for collecting and storing blood samples. The decision to move was influenced by the answers given by their management to the questions in Table 21.

Table 21 *Questions and answers of a firm considering moving to the South West.*

Why . . .	Because . . .
1 . . . do we need to build another factory?	. . . we cannot meet the increasing demand for our products from our existing factories.
2 . . . might we locate in Europe?	. . . we could then produce within the fast-growing market of Western Europe.
3 . . . choose South West England?	. . . the UK government gives financial and other help to firms setting up in Assisted Areas.
4 . . . opt for Devon?	. . . there are good transport links to the rest of our market area, and it is a pleasant area in which to live (fig. 6.14).
5 . . . site the factory on the northern outskirts of Plymouth?	. . . the environment is semi-rural, there is suitable land available, also enough labour with the skills required.

On the Belliver industrial estate they built a 20,000 m^2 showpiece factory, which had to blend in with the surroundings. Care was taken to landscape the site by adding trees, small bushes and flower beds. The factory is fully air-conditioned. A central computer controls both the working environment and the production line. The 400 employees have locker and changing rooms and a large cafeteria. The site has space for future expansion. Products are despatched by road transport throughout the UK and to the Channel ports for movement to continental Europe.

Fig. 6.14. What British Aerospace discovered when interviewing engineers for new jobs at Plymouth.

Fig. 6.15. Southern England's Silicon Strip.

Toshiba Corporation, with its headquarters in Tokyo, has two branch factories in Plymouth. One factory, opened in 1981 on the Ernesettle industrial estate, makes colour television sets and video recorders. To meet a newer and increasing demand for microwave ovens, another factory was opened four years later at Belliver – the same estate as selected by Becton Dickinson. Toshiba employs 1,000 people at the two Plymouth sites (worldwide it has 10,000 employees).

There can be some disadvantages in having within an area the branch factory of a large foreign firm. What might these be?

Silicon strip

Fig. 6.15 shows an extremely important corridor of growth industries in the UK. It stretches either side of the M4 from London to Swansea, via Swindon and Bristol. There is an extension southwest-wards along the M5 and A38 to Plymouth. Within this corridor have grown high-technology firms using microchips in their products, e.g. Digital, Ferranti, Honeywell and Logica. They also make software (programs) for computers.

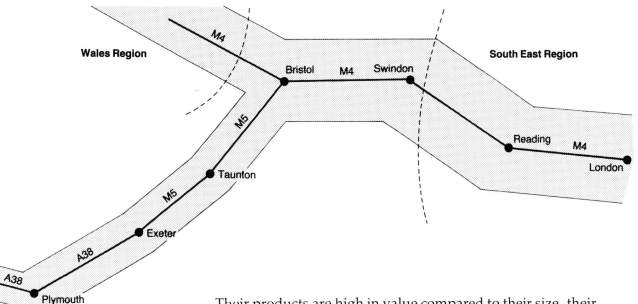

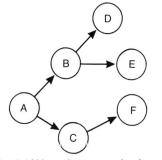

Fig. 6.16. 'A' is an innovator, i.e. has a new idea or technique. This spreads, or diffuses, very quickly to 'B'–'F' because they are all close to one another.

Their products are high in value compared to their size, their selling area is large (usually world-wide), and they need a very large number of skilled employees for their operations.

How could a location close to a motorway be a help to each of the three features just mentioned?

Once a corridor like this becomes established, its rôle as an area of high-technology activity becomes **accumulative**, that is it attracts to it an ever-increasing number of similar or linked activities. There are some firms which concentrate on developing new ideas or inventing new products. An ideal location for them is within a new type of estate known as a 'Science Park', close to a University or Polytechnic, e.g. at Bath and at Plymouth. This is a great advantage because new ideas and techniques can be **diffused** (or spread) quickly and easily at advanced levels of investigation around the Park (fig. 6.13).

The inflow of employees into expanding areas requires much extra housing. As a result, a planning conflict can arise. It is hard to turn away firms which can bring prosperity. However, this has to be weighed against the environmental and social effects which they could have.

Table 22 *Some factors influencing factory location.*

| | Type of factory | | | | | | | | | | | |
| | yoghurt | | | fashion shoes | | | heli- copter | | | farming fertilizer | | |
	VI	I	NI	VI	I	NI	VI	I	NI	VI	I	NI
1 all raw materials found nearby												
2 large supply of highly-skilled workers												
3 quick access to first-class roads												
4 'linkage firms' close by												
5 large area of flat land for factory buildings												
6 sales markets close at hand												
another very important influencing factor												

VI – very important; I – important; NI – not important

On a sheet of A4 paper, design a publicity hand-out poster which could be used as part of a campaign to attract firms to the South West.

Copy Table 22. For each of the six factors, decide whether it could be very important, important or not important in influencing the location of a factory making each of the four products. Put ticks in the relevant spaces. For each product, add one extra factor which could be very important for the present-day location of the factory.

Discuss with others in your teaching group the hypothesis that 'access to good transport systems is the most important factor in the success of manufacturing industry in South West England'.

Office jobs

All firms undertake office activities such as typing, filing, keeping accounts and telephoning. Larger businesses employ people trained especially for such tasks. However, there are firms which specialise in the office functions of publicity, accountancy, insurance and data collecting. Taken together, they form another 'growth activity' in the United Kingdom. They now employ more people than there are in manufacturing and processing.

This growth has taken place in three main forms. Some firms have occupied **purpose-built** high-rise office blocks in city centres (fig. 6.18). On other occasions a large individual office has been built on the outskirts of a city. A third form of development is the Business Park. This is designed for use by a number of office-function firms in single- or two-storey buildings with high-technology facilities, e.g. at Windmill Hill (Swindon), Langage (Plymouth) and Aztec West north of Bristol (fig. 6.17). Banks, shops, leisure and medical facilities are provided within the Parks for use by the employees. There is plenty of space for parking cars. The whole Park is landscaped to provide an attractive environment in which to work.

Fig. 6.17. The entrance sign to the 70 hectare Aztec West Business Park (Bristol).

Look at fig. 6.6 for its location, and note how close it is to the two motorways.

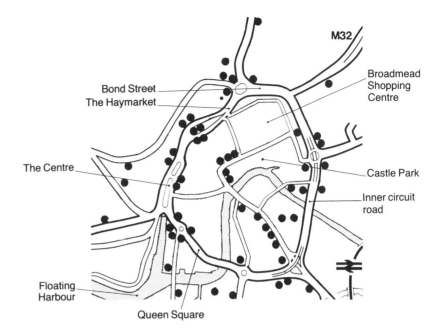

Fig. 6.18. The location of 30 office blocks in Central Bristol, which has more than 10 million km² of office space.

Bond Street
The Haymarket
M32
Broadmead Shopping Centre
The Centre
Castle Park
Inner circuit road
Floating Harbour
Queen Square

What are the advantages for office activities having
(a) a city centre location?
(b) new purpose-built premises?

Using electronics, information is now being put into digital form. This allows data to be processed speedily and transferred from place to place by means of advanced telecommunications (fig. 6.19). More and more people are now engaged in this type of work – almost one half of the South West's total employment in 1987.

Fig. 6.19. Processing and storing data electronically.

In addition to the jobs in offices of private firms, about 5% of the region's employees work in the offices of national government, e.g. taxation, defence, health and social security. For example, many work in the Admiralty Offices at Bath, while near Cheltenham is the Government Communications Headquarters where secret work is carried out. Some government offices have been moved away from London for the same reasons as have private firms. They have relocated in such large towns as Bristol (e.g. the Department of the Environment) and Plymouth (e.g. the Home Office). Other people work at lower levels of administration – in the offices of a County Council, a District Council or a local Town Hall.

All such employees are included in Employment Group 9 (Table 8). From this Table you can see that this Group has the highest percentage of any Group in the South West.

7 For rest and play

Boom, boom, boom

During the last twenty years, leisure activities have grown enormously. Several things have been responsible for this. In the first place, many people have become more affluent. As a person's wealth increases, the part which is seen as **disposable income** also increases. So these people demand more recreation, holidays and the like.

Secondly, the time which people have for recreation and leisure has also increased. Fig. 7.1 shows a gradual decrease in the length

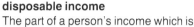

disposable income
The part of a person's income which is left after essential things have been bought. Only 2% of average incomes in 1950, it had risen to 18% by 1986.

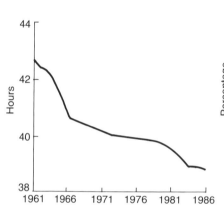

Fig. 7.1. Average weekly hours of work, excluding overtime, in the United Kingdom.

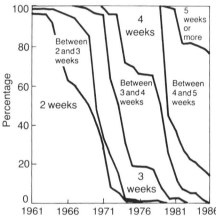

Fig. 7.2. The length of annual paid holiday in the UK.

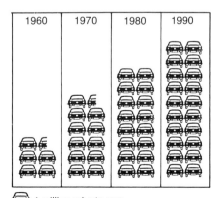

1 million private cars

Fig. 7.3. The number of people owning cars in the United Kingdom.

of the average working week from 45 hours in the 1950s to 40 hours by the mid 1980s. In 1960, 95% of those in full-time employment were entitled legally to only two weeks' paid holiday a year. By 1985, 80% of them were entitled to four weeks or more (fig. 7.2). People are retiring earlier, and, as we saw in Chapter 2, they are living longer. So again, there is more time available for leisure.

Thirdly, our society has become more mobile, especially as a result of increasing car ownership (fig. 7.3). This allows people to travel more easily when and where they like. Also, this added convenience has made 'touring around' an area a favourite activity during holidays and weekends.

The result of all these trends is that taking part in leisure and recreational activities has shifted from being a privilege for a few people, to an expected part of living for the majority.

Table 23 *The percentage of British holiday-makers visiting each of the English Tourist Board Regions in 1987.*

West Country	15
London	14
Heart of England	10
East Anglia	10
North West	9
Yorkshire and Humberside	8
South East	8
Southern	7
Thames and Chilterns	7
East Midlands	7
Northumbria	4
Cumbria	3

isochrone

A line joining all points which have the same value of time.

Top of the charts

The opportunities for leisure and recreation among the 4.5 million people living permanently in the South West have therefore grown. Yet, as Table 23 shows, the West Country is the top area chosen for holidays by people who live in Great Britain. In 1987, over 18 million holiday visits were made to the West Country.

Why must this last figure be increased in order to obtain the total number holidaying throughout the South West of England? (Comparing fig. 7.5 with the map on page 4 will offer a clue.)

The number of holiday visits has grown dramatically as the South West has become more **accessible** from other parts of Britain. Road improvements, especially the building of motorways, have meant that more and more people are able to reach the region within comfortable travelling times.

Study fig. 7.4. Before the motorways were built, what was the average driving time to Plymouth from Gloucester and Southampton? What towns does this **isochrone** pass through or near now that the M4 and M5 can be used?

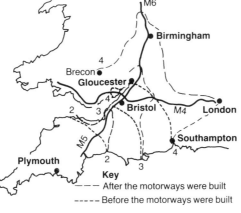

Fig. 7.4. Average driving times to Plymouth from southern Britain.

Table 24 *Fastest rail journey times in 1987.*

from London to	hrs	mins
Weston-super-Mare	2	1
Torquay	3	3
Penzance	4	46
Bournemouth	1	39
from Birmingham to		
Weston-super-Mare	2	8
Torquay	3	12
Penzance	5	26
Bournemouth	3	51

Fig. 7.5. The Regions of the English Tourist Board.

Within the area enclosed by the 4-hour isochrone live 20 million people. This is a vast number of possible customers desiring leisure and recreation in the South West – especially as the eastern and northern parts of this area contain some of the fastest growing populations in the whole of Britain. In addition, modern high-speed rail travel has greatly reduced journey times. Table 24 shows how short British Rail journeys can be, between two major centres of United Kingdom population and four holiday centres in the South West. Recent improvements in air linkage within Britain (Chapter 8) also allow people to reach the South West region more easily and quickly.

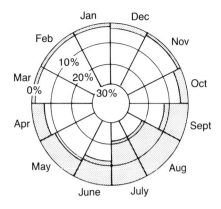

Fig. 7.6. When British people take their main holiday.

Why do they come?

Besides the better accessibility, is it the climate which draws so many people to the South West? In Chapter 1 we saw how people's perception of the region's climate matched up with the statistical data. Now let us focus our attention upon the summertime, since fig. 7.6 shows that this is the peak time for holidays. With July representing the summer period, let us test the **hypothesis** that 'resorts in the South West have a climatic advantage for a summer holiday over resorts elsewhere in Britain'.

Table 25 *Some features of the summer-time climate of some English resorts.*

		1	2	3	4	5	6	7
		total rainfall (mm)	total sunshine (hrs)	average temp (°C)				
A	Bournemouth	56	2139	21.4				
B	Torquay	55	2108	20.2				
C	Weston-s-Mare							
D	Blackpool							
E	Eastbourne							
F	Skegness							

Make a copy of Table 25, and using climatic data from an atlas,
(a) complete columns 1 to 3 for resorts C–F;
(b) in column 4, number the resorts in rank order of increasing total rainfall, giving '1' to the lowest total rainfall and '6' to the resort with the highest total;
(c) in columns 5 and 6, rank the resorts in order of descending total sunshine hours and descending average monthly temperatures, this time giving '1' to the highest totals;
(d) add up the numbers obtained by each resort in columns 4 to 6, and put this total rank score in column 7.

Which resort is 'best' (i.e. has the lowest total rank score)? Is it located in the South West? Do all the resorts outside of the South West have the highest total rank scores? Can we therefore support the hypothesis?

Is it the South West's environments which attract so many people? Fig. 7.7 illustrates three types of environment found within the region – coast, remote moorland and pretty village.

Fig. 7.7.

(a) Porthleven harbour, near Helston, Cornwall;

(b) the Blackbrook River meandering across Dartmoor near Princetown;

(c) Okeford Fitzpaine, near Blandford Forum in Dorset.

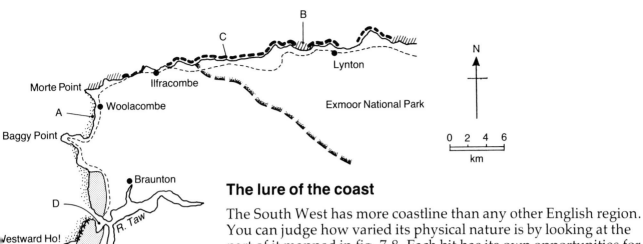

Fig. 7.8. Part of the coastline of North Devon.

	Sandy beach
	Rocky beach
	Pebble ridge
	Sand dunes
	High cliffs
	South West Peninsula Coast Path

The lure of the coast

The South West has more coastline than any other English region. You can judge how varied its physical nature is by looking at the part of it mapped in fig. 7.8. Each bit has its own opportunities for recreation.

Make a list of the leisure and recreational activities which it might be possible to undertake within a 4 km radius of each of the points labelled A, B, C and D in fig. 7.8. Consider activities using the land and the water, and include in each list at least one activity to interest (i) a teenager; (ii) an active middle-aged person; (iii) an elderly person. If you are able to study the Ordnance Survey 1:63,360 Tourist Map No. 5 of Exmoor, you could add more detail to your lists.

Groups of pupils compared beaches of the Lizard Peninsula. The way in which they gave a score to each beach is shown in Table 26. Also shown are the completed schedules for two of the beaches.

Table 26 *The things which were considered during a survey of beaches, and some of the results.*

	very good	good	adequate	poor	very poor	scores for beach A	beach B
access by car	5	4	3	2	1	2	4
amount of car parking	5	4	3	2	1	3	4
surface type	5 sand	4 shingle	3 pebble	2 rock		4	5
aspect	5 south		3 east or west		1 north	3	5
swimming conditions	5	4	3	2	1	4	3
absence of litter	5	4	3	2	1	5	3
number of facilities on or near to beach	5	4	3	2	1	2	4
Total score						23	28

weighting
Each feature is given a value which shows how important it is thought to be compared to the other features.

Why might beach B be preferred by a family of four (including two young children) having a holiday touring by car in Cornwall? If there is a beach near where you live, what scores would it get? Do you agree with the **weightings** used in the schedule? What other feature which could be scored would you like to add?

How the map changes

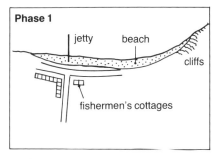

Phase 1
jetty   beach
cliffs
fishermen's cottages

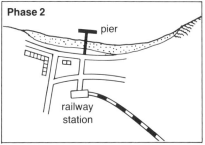

Phase 2
pier
railway station

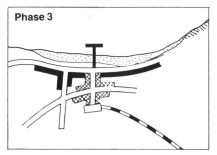

Phase 3

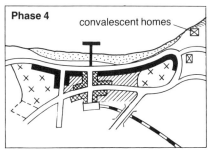

Phase 4
convalescent homes

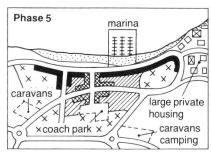

Phase 5
marina
caravans
large private housing
coach park
caravans camping

Key
Recreation Business District
Main area of shops and offices
Guest houses, Bed and Breakfast, private housing

Notes on the main features

A very small settlement, with houses for a few fishermen who obtain a living from coastal waters; small jetty helps to launch boats across the beach.

Two major buildings appear – railway station and pier, Victorian in style; the latter has amenities for mass recreation; most visitors are 'day trippers' from large inland towns.

A 'week's holiday' becomes fashionable; accommodation for this is built – for the wealthy, large hotels overlooking sea and spreading along promenade; guest-houses and bed-and-breakfast houses elsewhere; mainly 'sand-castles and bathing'; between railway station and pier grows an RBD (page 00).

Increasing numbers arrive by car and charabanc; the town centre expands to cater for both visitors and locals, whose main function is to look after visitors; convalescent homes built on higher areas with pleasant views and relative quietness.

Movement to coast now mainly by road; railway station closes; excursion platforms, sidings, etc. become car/coach park; caravan/camping sites along approach roads; hotels close or become holiday flats; entertainment styles change – pier decays, cinemas become bingo halls, water activities expand; large expensive houses on higher south-facing areas.

A resort's many faces

Fig. 7.9. A model of resort development.

68

So great is the demand for recreation at the coast that many resorts have grown up with a special purpose, or function, of looking after visitors. Most of them began to grow in the nineteenth century, when 'a visit to the seaside' became the popular family event of the year – an event made possible by the building of railways (e.g. to Teignmouth in 1846) and the selling of cheap rail excursion tickets. Often the resorts began life as fishing harbours, e.g. Mousehole, Brixham and Lyme Regis. Figure 7.9 is a model of resort development divided into five phases. It shows how a resort changes as a result of:

(a) increases in the demand for recreation;
(b) changes in the type of recreation demanded;
(c) changes in economic and social conditions.

Fig. 7.10. Weston-super-Mare (Avon).

Compare this sketch with Stage 5 of the Resort Model. What features are found in both? What differences are there?

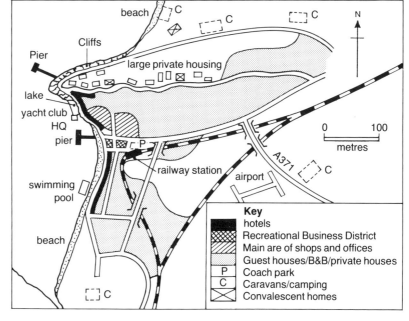

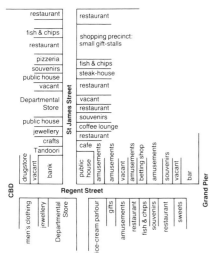

One major change in a resort's appearance is the development of a **Recreational Business District**. Its character can be judged from fig. 7.11.

Fig. 7.11. The ground-floor functions and a street-level view of part of the Recreational Business District of Weston-super-Mare.

Describe the features of this RBD.

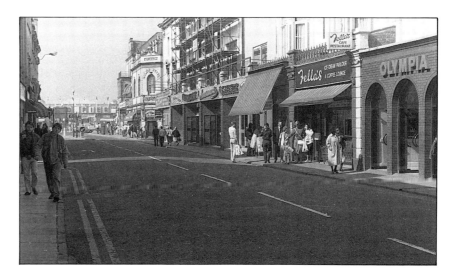

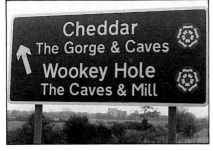

Fig. 7.12. (a) direction sign on the M5 motorway; it has the logo of the English Tourist Board; (b) moorland ponies and vegetation, Dartmoor

Inland honeypots – natural

Some of the features which attract people to the inland parts of the South West are shown in fig. 7.12. They include the beauty of the scenery, the appeal of the flora and fauna, and the chance of 'getting-away-from-it-all' into a peaceful environment.

During one day in the peak holiday season, surveys were carried out in one moorland environment.

kite flying
photography
paddling
picnicking
playing cricket
sketching
sun bathing
walking
writing postcards

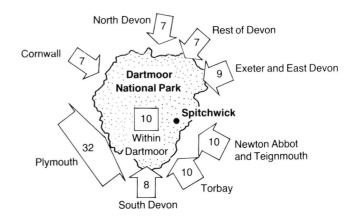

Fig. 7.13. The percentages of people who came from various directions to visit Dartmoor on Sunday 10 August 1986, and the activities being undertaken at 12 noon at the Spitchwick honeypot (marked on the map).

Sort these activities into each of the following two groups:
(a) formal (needing special provision/equipment) or informal;
(b) physically active or not physically active;
(c) can be undertaken best within 10 metres of where the car is parked, or further away from the car.

All of these activities require space, and enjoying one of them could interfere with someone else's enjoyment of another. Fig. 7.14 is a **compatibility** matrix. It shows the amount of interference which activities can have on others when undertaken at the same time in any one place.

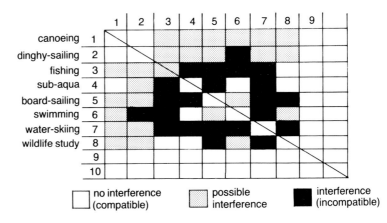

Fig. 7.14. This shows how compatible some water activities are with each other at a honeypot.

Copy the matrix. Add two activities of your choice, and then complete the matrix. Do you agree with the shadings? Are there any major disagreements (that is, where it is shown that two activities are compatible but you feel that they are incompatible and vice versa)?

Inland honeypots – human

Castle Combe

Castle Combe is a small Wiltshire village
Which lies in a wooded ravine,
With cottages made of grey limestone
And a river enhancing the scene.

To this 'prettiest village' in England
Come visitors daily to see
This tranquil old place with its 'Old Worlde' charm,
And learn of its past history.

Once known as a centre for weaving,
The weaver's house stands there, serene,
And the old Market Place is its focal point still,
With houses and Inns in between.

Completing this picturesque village
And looking as grand still today
Is its beautiful Church, Fifteenth Century built,
Where those folk long ago went to pray.

Fig. 7.15. A poem by Gwen Ellis. Small towns and villages built of local stone, like Castle Combe, attract many people

Fig. 7.16. (a) Stonehenge had 500,000 visitors in 1987; (b) the Roman Baths at Bath (830,000 visitors). English Heritage, a public organisation set up in 1984, is responsible for these and other locations in the South West.

Historical monuments and important homes and gardens (fig. 7.16) also attract. Some are privately-owned. Others are run by the National Trust or English Heritage. They are the favourites of visitors from overseas. In 1987 over 1.25 million people visited the West Country from abroad. Most came from the USA.

	number of visitors
Stourhead Gardens	183,000
St Michael's Mount	169,000
Corfe Castle	154,000
Lanhydrock	122,500
Brownsea Island	110,000
Kingston Lacy	108,000
Hidcote Gardens	96,500
Dunster Castle	90,000
Castle Drogo	85,500
Cotehele	83,000

Table 27 *1986's Top Ten properties in the SW owned by the National Trust. This is a private organisation looking after land, houses and their contents for the nations enjoyment.*

Fig. 7.17. Human skill can create honeypots, e.g. by preserving for the enjoyment of present-day visitors the working and living conditions of previous generations when they farmed (a), or mined for tin (b)

People converging upon the honeypots can cause congestion, especially when caravans and luxury coaches use minor country roads. We can see in fig. 7.18 an attempt made by the Dartmoor National Park Authority to reduce road congestion. Using such methods of management, the character of areas can be protected. Also, people's search for recreation can be channelled along routes and towards sites which are able to take them comfortably.

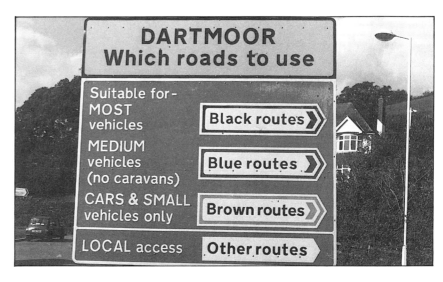

Fig. 7.18. A notice-board near Ashburton on a road approaching the Dartmoor National Park. Direction signs have the words and edges in different colours.

Fig. 7.19. Part of a hand-out describing Wiltshire's Cycleway.

Come and ride through the glorious countryside of Wiltshire and see rural England at its best!

The Wiltshire Cycleway follows mainly quiet country lanes, over rolling hills with spectacular views, through peaceful wooded valleys and past delightful towns and villages. There are famous prehistoric sites, magnificent stately homes, splendid gardens and a wealth of other attractions to visit en route.

Strong experienced cyclists could probably complete the 160 mile route in a weekend. If you are less energetic and want to discover Wiltshire's rich heritage, we suggest you have a more leisurely trip.

Cycling is a healthy way for the family to explore our countryside. Enjoy your ride in Wiltshire!

Fig. 7.20. The 'acorn' symbol is used to signpost long-distance footpaths. Set up by the Countryside Commission, with money from national government, these pathways allow people to walk long distances through areas of varied scenery, history and wildlife.

Corridors for leisure

(a) A century ago, the Kennet and Avon Canal flourished as a 140 km long industrial waterway linking Bristol and Reading. Following decades of non-use and neglect, sections of it have been cleared of weed and rubbish, and some locks restored. This has given it a new life as a waterway for pleasure craft.

(b) Some branch railway lines, closed in the 1960s because they were uneconomic, have also been restored as tourist attractions by enthusiastic volunteer groups – for example the Dart Valley Steam Railway between Buckfastleigh and Totnes. Elsewhere, where the rail track was removed, e.g. between Barnstaple and Bideford, the routes have been made into official walkways or cycle tracks.

(c) Wiltshire County Council has encouraged enjoyment of the countryside by creating a Cycleway around some of the county's places of interest (fig. 7.19). Linking up with a bus company, Devon County Council has promoted a summertime 'Transmoor Link'. This enables people to enjoy moorland views from a double-decker bus between Exeter and Plymouth across Dartmoor. It also gives access to starting-points for those wishing to walk across the open moorland at leisure.

(d) Being 830 km long, the South West Peninsula Coast Path is the longest long-distance footpath in the British Isles. It hugs the coast from Minehead to Poole, and part of it is shown on fig. 7.8. By using it, walkers can enjoy such varied scenes as high moorlands in Somerset and North Devon, smugglers' coves in Cornwall, drowned river valleys in South Devon and chalk cliffs in Dorset.

Balance of Payments

A country's annual balance sheet, with the cost of things bought from abroad in one column, and the income from goods sold overseas in another column. Tourism is an important item 'sold' to foreign countries.

Table 28 *How much visitors spent and how many were employed in looking after them in the West Country in 1986.*

Spending		
by British visitors		£1055 million
by overseas visitors		£ 206 million

Employment	males	females
in hotels and catering	33,310	68,500
in recreation and leisure	24,970	21,800

Fig. 7.22. Devon Cliffs Holiday Camp, East Devon.

urban morphology

The physical make-up of a town – its roads, buildings and open spaces.

Profit or loss?

Undertaking leisure and recreational activities usually costs money. Not surprisingly therefore, the South West benefits greatly from all the spending of its visitors (Table 28). Foreign tourists are highly sought after. They help Britain's **Balance of Payments**. The benefits can come *directly* or *indirectly*, and the financial ones are shown in fig. 7.21.

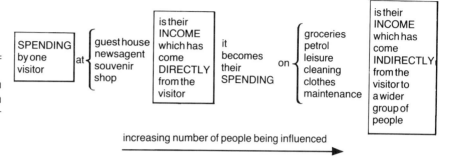

Fig. 7.21. A model of the financial benefits of tourism.

Draw a diagram similar to this to show the other major economic benefit to the SW – direct and indirect employment.   0

There are, however, disadvantages in being so popular. Conflict can arise over using land for recreation rather than for other purposes. The problem of traffic congestion was mentioned on page 72. Salcombe, in South Devon, with 2,500 local residents, has its population swollen to 12,000 in midsummer. This puts a strain on water supplies (see fig. 4.16), and police and medical services, which are expensive to provide. They have to be paid for by permanent residents – even though they may be used fully for only part of the year.

Should a limit be placed on the number of people visiting an area? If so, how could this be carried out, and who should make the decisions?

Another disadvantage is that much employment in hotels, catering and leisure services is lowly-paid. It is also highly seasonal. Resorts, bustling in the summer, are places of high unemployment during the winter. Attempts are being made to extend the length of the holiday season, for example by encouraging low-priced package coach holidays in the spring and autumn. At Bournemouth and Torquay, new Conference/ Exhibition Centres have been built to attract large international gatherings. Being open all the year round, the Centres bring not just direct permanent employment, but a wide range of indirect employment as well.

Finally, there is visual impact. The trend towards more informal self-catering leisure is seen throughout the region. In the towns, holiday flats have been purpose built (see page 00) or made by converting hotels. In these ways, the **urban morphology** is changed. Elsewhere, caravan or camping sites develop (fig. 7.22). Without some control on their growth, they can become an eyesore in the very environment which visitors have come to enjoy.

Lines and links

Routes overland

The long peninsular shape, indented coastline and varied relief of the South West have always presented special difficulties to the builders of roads and railways across the region. Having to overcome these problems has made the network more costly to construct and maintain.

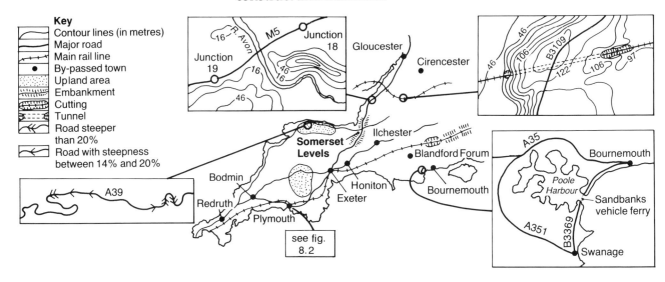

Key
- ▬ Contour lines (in metres)
- ▬ Major road
- ┼┼┼ Main rail line
- • By-passed town
- ░ Upland area
- ▨ Embankment
- ▨ Cutting
- ▨ Tunnel
- ↞ Road steeper than 20%
- ↞ Road with steepness between 14% and 20%

Fig. 8.1. The lines of some major east–west routes across the peninsula. The towns which are marked are some of those which have been by-passed by new major roads.

Referring to the map above, and the one on page 4, re-write Table 29 by matching each problem with its solution. (One has already been done for you.)

Table 29 *Some problems faced by the route planners, and how they decided to overcome them.*

Some required routes and the problems	Some solutions
From London (Paddington) to Bristol via Swindon by main line railway through the hills of Wiltshire.	Building embankments made of local limestone and South Wales mining waste.
Building a Motorway across the Somerset Levels which are liable to flood.	A six-lane low-level bridge for the M5 Motorway.
By car from Bournemouth to Swanage by the shortest route.	A winding route with steep gradients up to 25% across Exmoor.
A main road across NW Somerset and N Devon where only a narrow coastal plain exists.	A 3 km-long tunnel at Box, just east of Bath.
From Exeter to Plymouth by main road and rail; Dartmoor lies between these towns.	Making deep cuttings and long embankments.
Crossing the broad valley of the River Avon by motorway, west of Bristol.	A 400 m vehicle ferry across the entrance to Poole harbour.
From London (Waterloo) to Exeter via Salisbury by main line railway across the chalklands of Wiltshire.	Increasing the length of the routes so that the gradients are gentle ones.

Fig. 8.2. Old (1859) and new (1966) routes linking Devon with Cornwall across the estuary of the River Tamar.

Fig. 8.3. The car park at Tiverton Parkway can be used by commuters living within a very large surrounding (or catchment) area.

Some of the problems were solved a long time ago. It was in the mid-nineteenth century that the Clifton Suspension Bridge across the Avon Gorge and the Tamar rail bridge were built by Brunel, and the Severn estuary was tunnelled for a rail line. However, another 100 years and more passed before these three rivers were bridged for extra road links. When the Severn Bridge was opened in 1966, the region's links with South Wales were greatly improved. The journey by road between Bristol and Newport was shortened by 80 km.

How much time and money is saved by using this shorter route, if a car averages 80 kph, does 10 km per litre of petrol, and petrol costs 37 pence per litre? (There is a toll of 50p for crossing the bridge by car.)

Linking small and scattered communities is costly, because a very dense network of minor roads is needed. Devon has to keep in order 14,000 km of road. This is 3,500 km more than any other British county. Fewer passengers and less freight move by rail than by road in the South West. However, services on the main line railways have become high-speed. 125 Inter-City trains link the main centres of population. In order to attract long-distance commuters, Parkway Stations have been built at Bodmin, Bristol and Tiverton (figs. 6.3 and 8.3).

Coping with change

Increases in the amount of commercial and private traffic passing through towns and villages have caused problems. Movement has become difficult, slow, and dangerous to both people and buildings. These settlements need to be by-passed. Fig. 8.1 shows some locations where this has happened.

Deciding on the line of a new routeway can cause further conflict. If agreement cannot be reached easily, a long and costly **Public Inquiry** has to be held. At this meeting all points of view can be aired. Many years can therefore pass between the first proposals for a new route and the beginning of actual construction (fig. 8.4).

Fig. 8.4. Two possible routes to by-pass Okehampton. The Inquiry lasted 95 days. Eight years later, in 1988, the road was opened (the green route).

What groups of people would have wanted to state their views at the Public Inquiry before the actual route was chosen? What points of view might each group have put forward?

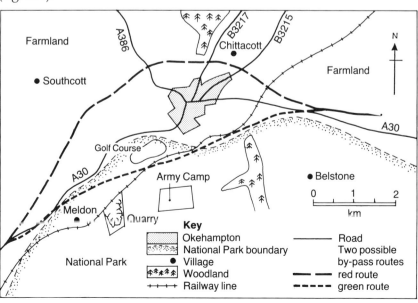

75

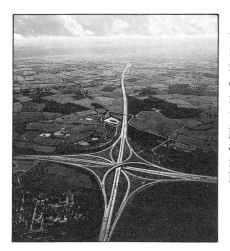

Fig. 8.5. Almondsbury, the meeting of the M4 and M5 motorways in Avon. Each kilometre of six-lane motorway uses 16 hectares of land. Interchanges and Service Areas also occupy large areas.

Following the closing in the 1960s of rail-lines which were unprofitable, many parts of the South West felt 'cut-off' from the rest of Britain. A 75 km North Devon Link Road is an attempt to increase that area's accessibility from the M5 motorway. When complete it will link Bideford, Barnstaple and Tiverton to the motorway close to Tiverton Parkway. This creates an ideal transport junction. Planners see the area surrounding this junction as one of great future growth (fig. 10.2). New housing and sites for manufacturing and distributing firms are growing fast. Modern road-building consumes very large quantities of land, as fig. 8.5 shows. Often these areas were formerly farmland.

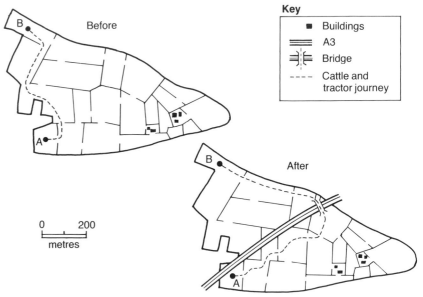

Fig. 8.6. This new route for the A31 north of Bournemouth has brought headaches to the owner of Staplehill Farm, Ferndown. He now finds that moving cattle and making journeys by tractor take longer and are more difficult, e.g. from A to B.

SUMMER 1988
DESTINATIONS

Balearic Islands
- Ibiza
- Majorca

Canary Islands
- Tenerife

Channel Islands
- Guernsey
- Jersey

France
- Dinard
- Paris

Spain
- Malaga

Portugal
- Faro

Yugoslavia
- Pula
- Split

Great Britain
- Belfast
- Isles of Scilly
- London (Gatwick)
- Plymouth

EXETER AIRPORT

Fig. 8.7. In 1988, Exeter had regular air links with these locations.

Routes above ground

The South West has many airports. Some, e.g. Gloucester–Cheltenham and Newquay, are relatively small. They cater for the need to move around a large region at a speed not possible by overland routes. To pay their way, most of these airports are also bases for recreational flying and gliding.

The larger airports at Bristol, Bournemouth, Exeter and Plymouth, have **charter and scheduled links** with the rest of the United Kingdom and overseas. Three groups of passengers benefit most from these links:

(a) business executives moving between company offices in this country and abroad;
(b) residents of the South West holidaying in the Channel Islands or the Mediterranean countries;
(c) people living elsewhere in the UK taking holidays in the South West.

Air/sea rescue along the South West's coastline and in the Bristol and English Channels depends upon military helicopters operating from Culdrose and St Mawgan in west Cornwall, Chivenor in north Devon and Portland in south Dorset.

Across the waters – goods

The nature of the coastline of South West England has always encouraged movement by sea. Numerous small ports and docks exist around the coast, e.g. at Sharpness, Teignmouth and Watchet. In the nineteenth century, Bristol was one of Great Britain's most important seaports (page 56). Silting up of the Avon estuary, the increasing size of vessels and the growth of **containerised traffic**, forced the city's docks to close. Substitutes were built at Avonmouth and Portbury (fig. 8.8).

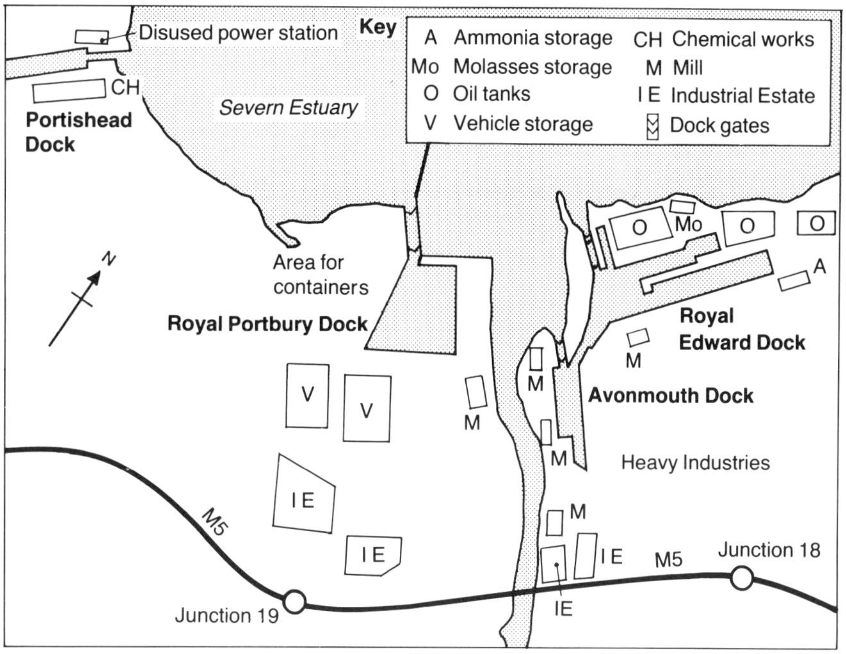

Key

A	Ammonia storage	CH	Chemical works
Mo	Molasses storage	M	Mill
O	Oil tanks	I E	Industrial Estate
V	Vehicle storage	⋈	Dock gates

Fig. 8.8. Vessels up to 30,000 tonnes can reach Avonmouth Docks. Portbury, opened in 1978, has six berths for 70,000 tonners. 1,000 hectares of adjoining land are used for the storage, handling and distribution of cargo.

There are two storage buildings for 'molasses' shown in fig. 8.8. What are 'molasses'?

Fig. 8.9. The Log for Exmouth Dock for a week in 1988. It closed in 1990.

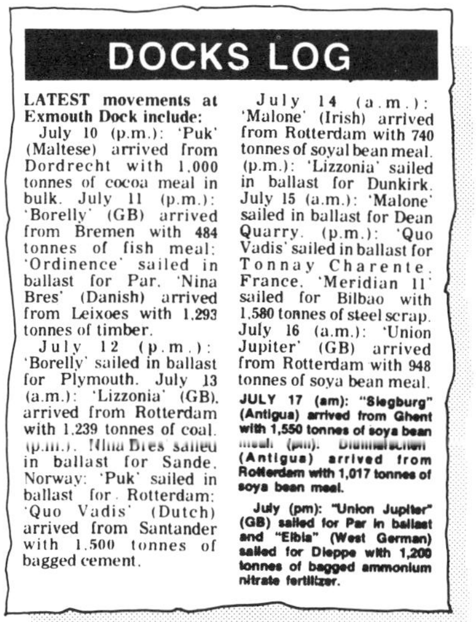

DOCKS LOG

LATEST movements at Exmouth Dock include:
July 10 (p.m.): 'Puk' (Maltese) arrived from Dordrecht with 1,000 tonnes of cocoa meal in bulk. July 11 (p.m.): 'Borelly' (GB) arrived from Bremen with 484 tonnes of fish meal; 'Ordinence' sailed in ballast for Par. 'Nina Bres' (Danish) arrived from Leixoes with 1,293 tonnes of timber.
July 12 (p.m.): 'Borelly' sailed in ballast for Plymouth. July 13 (a.m.): 'Lizzonia' (GB) arrived from Rotterdam with 1,239 tonnes of coal. (p.m.): 'Nina Bres' sailed in ballast for Sande, Norway; 'Puk' sailed in ballast for Rotterdam; 'Quo Vadis' (Dutch) arrived from Santander with 1,500 tonnes of bagged cement.

July 14 (a.m.): 'Malone' (Irish) arrived from Rotterdam with 740 tonnes of soyal bean meal. (p.m.): 'Lizzonia' sailed in ballast for Dunkirk. July 15 (a.m.): 'Malone' sailed in ballast for Dean Quarry. (p.m.): 'Quo Vadis' sailed in ballast for Tonnay Charente, France. 'Meridian 11' sailed for Bilbao with 1,580 tonnes of steel scrap. July 16 (a.m.): 'Union Jupiter' (GB) arrived from Rotterdam with 948 tonnes of soya bean meal.
JULY 17 (am): "Siegburg" (Antigua) arrived from Ghent with 1,550 tonnes of soya bean meal. (pm): 'Drummelachen' (Antigua) arrived from Rotterdam with 1,017 tonnes of soya bean meal.

July (pm): "Union Jupiter" (GB) sailed for Par in ballast and "Elbia" (West German) sailed for Dieppe with 1,200 tonnes of bagged ammonium nitrate fertilizer.

Read fig. 8.9 and list the cargoes handled at Exmouth Dock. Put them into groups, and mark the exported items with an 'E'. What is 'ballast'? Draw a sketch map to show the ports to which Exmouth was linked during that week in 1988. Now write a description of the features of Exmouth's trade which your groupings and map reveal.

Falmouth, Plymouth and Poole also have port facilities for handling a variety of large international cargoes. Special container services by road and rail connect these ports to places throughout Great Britain. Fowey and Par are specialist ports. The annual export of about 2 million tonnes of china clay from their hinterland is their main activity (see page 38).

Across the waters – people

Sending early-season market gardening produce (artichokes, cauliflowers and potatoes) by lorry to the British markets, was the original reason for having a cross-channel link between Roscoff in Brittany and Millbay (Plymouth). In 1987, 18,500 lorries used this route. So did 380,000 passengers and their cars. They used the Brittany Ferries as a tourist link between the UK and France or Spain. A new £5 million terminal at Millbay could double these figures in the near future.

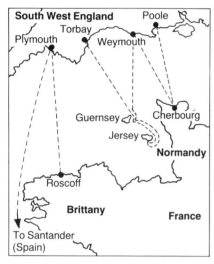

Fig. 8.10. Cross-channel routes linking the South West with the continent of Europe and the Channel Islands.

Table 30 *Three ways of linking the Isles of Scilly to West Cornwall across 45 km of water.*

from	by	journey time	number of passengers	number of return journeys each day	adult fare* during the summer (1988)
Penzance heliport	helicopter	20 mins	32	6–10	£33 day return £54 period return
Penzance harbour	boat ('Scillonian')	$2\frac{1}{2}$ hrs	600	1–2	£19 day return £35 period return
Land's End aerodrome	skybus	15 mins	10	5–10	£27 day return £42 period return

*reduced fares for children under 16.

Giving your reasons, decide which of the links in Table 30 is the one likely to be used by each of the following:
(a) a couple on a 5-day honeymoon visit;
(b) a teaching group on a 10-day field study visit;
(c) a grocery wholesaler sending a large load of breakfast cereals;
(d) a Scilly Island resident having an appointment at the nearest main hospital, at Penzance.

Links through space

The Lizard Peninsula has an important role in sending messages over long distances. In 1901 Marconi showed how 'wire-less' signals could be sent through the air to North America. To do this, a transmitter was built at Poldhu. Sixty years later, large dish aerials at Goonhilly began receiving and sending information via satellites orbiting the earth. People can now telephone friends and business colleagues or see television pictures of news events or sporting attractions at places throughout the world, by means of this Earth Satellite Station (fig. 8.11).

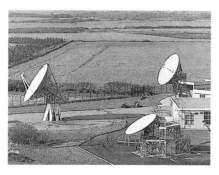

Fig. 8.11. Some of the ten dish aerials at Earth Satellite Station, Goonhilly, on the Lizard Peninsula. It operates 24 hours a day throughout the year.

Lines overhead

With the exception of small workings in the Forest of Dean and north east Avon, the South West has had no coalfields to meet demands for power within the region. Coal and oil have been imported, e.g. at the BP terminals at Bridgwater (Somerset) and Yelland in north Devon. Around the coast power stations were built to convert these **fossil fuels** into electricity, at Hayle, Plymouth and Portishead, for example. But these buildings are now disused (fig. 8.12) as a result of competition from other sources of energy.

fossil fuels
The remains of plants and animals which over millions of years have been changed into coal, oil or natural gas. They can be used only once.

Fig. 8.12. The former coal-fired power station beside the estuary of the River Plym.

Fig. 8.13. The location of the power stations and major lines of distribution within the region. Berkeley, the world's first nuclear power station, is now at the end of its working life.

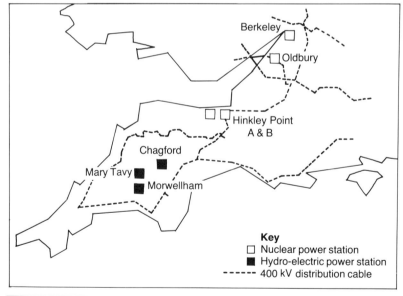

Key
☐ Nuclear power station
■ Hydro-electric power station
----- 400 kV distribution cable

Table 31 *How much electricity each power station can produce.*

Power station	type	output in MW
Berkeley	nuclear	334
Hinkley Point 'A'	nuclear	543
Hinkley Point 'B'	nuclear	1220
Oldbury	nuclear	458
Chagford	hydro	
Mary Tavy	hydro	3
Morwellham	hydro	

MW = megawatt = one million watts

renewable resources
Resources that can be used over and over again, like water, and heat from the sun.

CEGB
Central Electricity Generating Board, responsible for making and distributing electricity in England and Wales.

One competing source of energy is water, a **renewable resource**. As you can see from Table 31, the group of three hydro-electric power stations produce only a small amount of electricity. Because of this, their future is uncertain. Another competitor is uranium. It is imported from Canada and used for producing nuclear power. The South West has four of the **CEGB**'s ten nuclear power stations. They each produce large amounts of

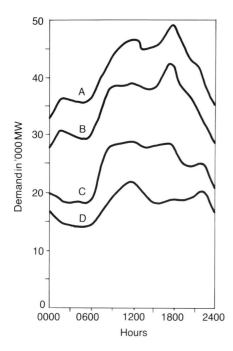

Fig. 8.14. The changes in demand for electricity in England and Wales on
A – a very cold day in winter;
B – a normal winter's day;
C – a normal summer's day;
D – a very hot day in summer.

Fig. 8.15. The part played by each type of power station in meeting the demand for electricity on a normal day in winter.

Table 32 *Merit Table*

1	nuclear
2	oil-fired
3	large coal-fired
4	small coal-fired
5	hydro
6	gas-fired

The most economic power stations are at the top. At any one time, the cheapest are operated first. As demand increases, the next most economic type is used, and so on until total demand is met.

electricity. They do, however, give rise to worry and controversy, especially over possible mishaps during operation. This happened at Chernobyl in the USSR in 1986, with widespread after-effects.

Radioactive fuel has an active life of seven years. After that, it is removed carefully from the reactor and left to cool in specially designed tanks. It is then transported by rail in 50-tonne steel containers to Sellafield in Cumbria for re-processing. The possibility of accidents while the waste is being handled and transported causes further concern.

A nuclear station at Winfrith is used for research purposes only.

A network of lines

Electricity cannot be stored. Yet you can see from fig. 8.14 that demand can change suddenly. The time of day, the weather conditions or a favourite television programme can cause this.

Refer to fig. 8.14. What causes the steep rise in demand between 07.00 and 09.00 hours? Why is there normally another peak between 17.00 and 18.00 hours? and why does this not occur in D? What could be responsible for the differences in the general levels and peaks of B and C?

The CEGB has to overcome these variations in demand. They do this by operating the coal- and oil-fired stations below their full capacity. Then if there is a sudden surge in demand, the output of these stations can be increased. Hydro-electric power stations can be 'switched on' to produce electricity at a moment's notice.

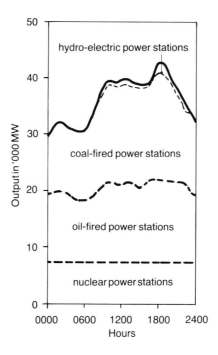

Fig. 8.15 shows that the output from nuclear power stations is continuous. They are supplying what is known as the **base load** of electricity. They are the cheapest to run as Table 32 indicates. The other types of station supply the **peaks** of demand.

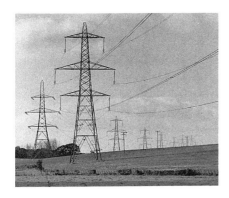

Fig. 8.16. Iron giants striding across East Devon. The cables and pylons from which they are hung are often very noticeable. Burying the cables underground is 15 times more expensive.

Early power stations were small and supplied just the area surrounding them. Since 1933, a network of power lines has been strung across the country (fig. 8.16). These high-voltage cables allow power to be distributed further away from larger producing stations. Each power station is now linked to this **grid system**. So a sudden increase in demand for electricity in the South West can be met by increasing the output of the coal-fired power stations in the Midlands.

There were plans to build a third nuclear power station at Hinkley Point, where 1,400 permanent staff are already employed. It would cost £1,500 million, and be able to produce 1,320kW of electricity more cheaply than any other power station.

Fig. 8.17. The nuclear power stations at Hinkley Point and the proposed site for the third one.

Write a letter to the editor of your local weekly newspaper, explaining as fully as you can the reasons why you would *either* wholeheartedly support the building of a nuclear power station 30 km from your home, *or* strongly oppose it.

Beneath land and sea

Natural gas has become a major source of power. A network of underground pipes distributes it from gasfields in the North Sea off the coast of East Anglia. Once the pipes are buried, the routes of the pipelines are hardly seen. Land on top of them can be used for farming and forestry. The network has not yet reached some parts of rural Cornwall. It is costly and difficult to link the small and scattered communities there.

Widemouth in North Cornwall will become the start of the world's most advanced undersea communications network. It will link Great Britain to France and North America. Using 6,600 km of **optic fibre cable**, the system will allow the sending of telephone calls and television pictures in digital form.

optic fibre cable
An advanced technology cable as thin as a hair, but which can carry hundreds of pieces of information such as words, pictures and sounds.

9 Town and country values

Loosening the rural grip

rural
Having links with a countryside which has no large towns within it.

Today, 30% of the South West's population is classified as **rural**. 100 years ago, the percentage was 60%. At that time a thriving agriculture and other activities in Employment Group 0 (see Table 8) gave full employment in the countryside. Most of the services needed, for example baker, blacksmith and school, were available locally. Other services were provided at a small town nearby. These developed the important function of a market town, where goods and services could be bought and sold, e.g. at Stow-on-the-Wold in Gloucestershire and Marlborough in Wiltshire.

Fig. 9.1. Evidence today of former prosperity and community function: the Yarn Market at Dunster, West Somerset.

Tonight's Power In The Land programme on ITV focuses on the Cotswold hamlet of Broadwell which dates back to before the Domesday Book and reports that its death knell has already been tolled by the recent closure of the village school because of falling rolls.
"When the school goes, that is the death of the village; the next thing is the pub, then the shop. Then the community spirit evaporates."
In the village, population 250, local young people are being forced out as they can't afford to buy homes.
Broadwell's loss of identity is just part of a national trend which is especially striking in Gloucestershire which has lost almost a quarter of its village schools in the past five years.

Fig. 9.2. A report about a 1988 television programme which showed the decline of a village in Gloucestershire.

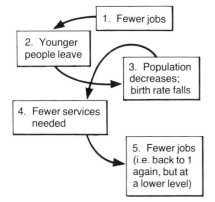

Fig. 9.3. A summary of the downward spiral of decline in rural areas.

But as time went by, the size and importance of rural communities declined. The teenagers and young adults left in search of employment in larger towns, so not only was there a loss of people, but the rural areas lost those younger persons who could create families in the future. Schools closed; bus services were not used; the village stores became what the naturalist David Bellamy has called 'an endangered species'.

What is meant by the words 'an endangered species'? Why are they words which a naturalist might choose to use?

Fig. 9.2 tells us that rural areas still have these sorts of problems today, and fig. 9.3 is one way of showing the decline.

Looking to the towns

Improvements in communications and increasing car ownership have made it easier for people to journey into the towns, not just for employment but also for shopping.

A teaching group enquired into what goods and services were available for the population living within a small area of Devon. After discussion, it was decided to limit their enquiry to fifteen types of goods and services. For data, they used the addresses (not the telephone exchange names) given in copies of the Exeter Yellow Pages Directory. Working in groups, they counted the number of times each type of activity was listed within the study area. Their results were pooled and some of them are included in Table 33. This shows both the variety and the number of shops and services available. Also shown are some of the conclusions which they drew from the enquiry.

Table 33 *Some of the goods and services which can be found in Tiverton and three nearby settlements in central Devon.*

	numbers of goods and services found in:			
	Bickleigh	Willand	Cullompton	Tiverton
general store		2	10	13
post office	1	1	2	4
public house	1	2	4	14
primary school	1	1	2	13
secondary school			2	4
further education college				1
police station			1	1
supermarket			3	4
estate agent			6	6
travel agent			1	3
bank			4	6
chemist			2	4
library			1	1
sports centre				1
hospital				2
size of population	200	2,000	5,000	17,000

These are **low-order** centres. They provide goods and services which people need most often and for which they are not prepared to travel far. The goods and services are known as **convenience** items. The sellers have comparatively small incomes, and they operate from comparatively small shops or offices.

Higher-order centres. Goods and services are needed less often. People are happy to travel further for them. There are many comparison shops, where people can shop around to compare similar items. These centres have a wide **sphere of influence**, i.e. they attract customers from a wide area. The businesses are often large.

A resident of Willand sees advantages in shopping at the local general stores instead of at the supermarket at Cullompton. What advantages could these be?

Why is there no secondary school at Willand?

Why is Tiverton the only settlement in the area with a hospital?

Why might using Yellow Pages not give absolutely accurate results? Can you think of a more accurate method which might be used if you were to investigate an area near where you live?

For this type of enquiry, using actual addresses is better than using the names of the telephone exchanges. Why?

Stemming the tide

Certain actions have been taken to try to stop people leaving the rural areas. For example, goods and services are brought to the customer instead of the customer having to do the travelling. The mobile grocer and greengrocer bring regular produce to the homes of rural families in the South West. Once a week, or every fortnight, library vans visit points which are convenient stopping-places for each community (fig. 9.4).

Fig. 9.4. One of the timetables of the Exe Library van. It allows people who live in parts of East Devon to use the services of a library once every two weeks. A library is a service usually located only in a town.

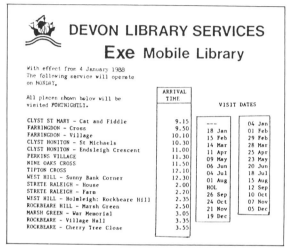

DEVON LIBRARY SERVICES
Exe Mobile Library

With effect from 4 January 1988
The following service will operate
on MONDAY.

All places shown below will be
visited FORTNIGHTLY.

	ARRIVAL TIME	VISIT DATES	
CLYST ST MARY - Cat and Fiddle	9.15	---	04 Jan
FARRINGDON - Cross	9.50	18 Jan	01 Feb
FARRINGDON - Village	10.10	15 Feb	29 Feb
CLYST HONITON - St Michaels	10.30	14 Mar	28 Mar
CLYST HONITON - Endsleigh Crescent	11.00	11 Apr	25 Apr
PERKINS VILLAGE	11.30	09 May	23 May
NINE OAKS CROSS	11.50	06 Jun	20 Jun
TIPTON CROSS	12.10	04 Jul	18 Jul
WEST HILL - Sunny Bank Corner	12.30	01 Aug	15 Aug
STRETE RALEIGH - House	2.00	HOL	12 Sep
STRETE RALEIGH - Farm	2.20	26 Sep	10 Oct
WEST HILL - Holmleigh: Rockbeare Hill	2.35	24 Oct	07 Nov
ROCKBEARE HILL - Marsh Green	2.50	21 Nov	05 Dec
MARSH GREEN - War Memorial	3.05	19 Dec	
ROCKBEARE - Village Hall	3.35		
ROCKBEARE - Cherry Tree Close	3.55		

The postbus is a salvation to areas which have lost their bus services. The daily delivery of mail is combined with carrying people to other villages or to the town from which the postal service operates (figs. 9.5 and 9.6).

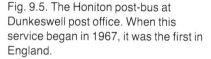

Fig. 9.5. The Honiton post-bus at Dunkeswell post office. When this service began in 1967, it was the first in England.

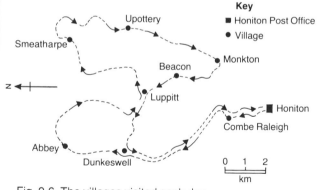

Fig. 9.6. The villages visited each day by the post-bus during its afternoon journey. When it is needed, it also stops at any farm or cottage along its route.

Injecting new blood

Rural areas in the South West are now regarded as attractive places in which to live, so much so that since 1971 their population numbers have started to increase. People are preferring to live in the countryside while continuing to work in the towns. They are known as commuters. Better transport links allow this separation of homeplace and workplace.

The alteration, improvement and modernisation of property have brought a new look and new life to many villages. Fig. 9.7 shows three buildings which have had their previous functions changed into permanent living accommodation. The changes have given extra direct employment opportunities to local builders, plumbers and electricians. Extra income has also come indirectly to those providing other services.

Who might benefit indirectly from this extra income?

Fig. 9.7. Some rural buildings which have been converted into houses: (a) a chapel near Penzance.
What would have been the previous use of (b), which is near Barnstaple? What features in the photograph helped you to make your decision?

Isolated and neglected rural cottages have been given a new value as **second homes**, particularly by those living in urban areas. The official definition of a second home is 'a property owned or rented which is used as an occasional home by a household which usually lives elsewhere'. If these properties were built before 1900, they often lack the three amenities regarded as basic to present-day living standards – bathroom, inside WC and piped cold water. When rebuilt and modernised, they become highly-desired properties. They are often bought because they are set in peaceful and beautiful countryside. Their owners are therefore likely to be very keen on preserving these two features. In some parts of North Cornwall and South Devon, nearly every property in a village has become a second home.

These settlements are sometimes called 'ghost villages'. Why and when might this happen?

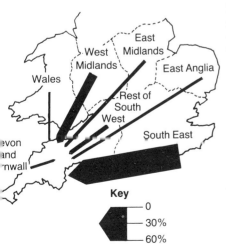

Key
— 0
— 30%
— 60%

Fig. 9.8. The usual home locations of those households having second-homes in Cornwall or Devon.

Write a paragraph which includes the ideas of 'size of population', 'personal wealth' and 'transport links' to suggest possible reasons for the pattern shown on the map.

Fig. 9.9. Points of view for and against people having second-homes in a village.

Think of two extra opinions which you would add to each side of this drawing.

Fig. 9.10. A former mill in the village of Tuckenhay, near Totnes. It made high-quality hand-made paper. Closed in 1960, it remained disused for many years. It is now divided into 15 holiday apartments. Nearby, mill workers' cottages have also been converted into leisure accommodation, bringing new life into the village.

Fig. 9.11. Luxury timeshare lodges in the parkland of a large private country estate near Camborne, West Cornwall.

Timeshare is another way in which larger rural property has been given a new life and a new value. People buy one or two weeks' share of the modernised property over a long period of time. This gives them an annual luxury holiday in the property and its surroundings, which are 'theirs' for that week or two.

Why might it be better to have 'timeshare' rather than 'second home' properties within a community?

So great have been the changes in people's perception of rural areas, that the trend is now for second home and timeshare properties to be purpose-built rather than just conversions of existing buildings (fig. 9.11).

Unless they are carefully planned, all these changes can destroy the former rural way of life. The moving-in of too many people can alter the very peaceful environment which they are seeking.

Fig. 9.12. Part of a pamphlet which advertises a Leisure Farm near Launceston, Cornwall.

Fig. 9.13. A road-sign to persuade motorists who are approaching Exeter to leave their cars at the outskirts of the city.

Fig. 9.14. Brunel Centre, Swindon. Shops and other services have been put entirely under cover, to provide dry, warm and pleasant surroundings in which to shop.

Also, the inflow of people used to an **urban** way of life can lead to conflicts of opinion and attitude within a community. A 'them' and 'us' situation may arise.

What is this rural life?

We saw in Chapter 5 that farmers need to use their land for other purposes. Forming a Country Park is one way of doing this. Set up on the fringes of large towns, they mix farming life with opportunities for leisure and recreation. Urban visitors can practise horse-riding or make a study of rare breeds of animals. Leisure Farms allow people to appreciate the everyday working of a farm. Visitors are encouraged to 'try their hand' at farm activities such as milking or tractor driving (fig. 9.12). In ways such as these it is hoped that bridges will be built between the outlooks and values of the rural and urban ways of life.

Look back at fig. 9.3. If we want to stop the spiral developing, we have to break into it at some point. Look at each of the stages 1 to 4, and consider what action could be taken at that stage, and by whom, to break into the spiral. Would it cost any money to take this action? If so, who should pay?

Bringing rural values into the town

Many people give a high value to lots of open space and little traffic. Some town centres have become **pedestrian precincts**. They are safer and quieter environments. However, for them to exist, enough parking-space has to be provided somewhere. Large multi-storey car parks are sometimes built close to the town centre. From them, people are able to walk to the shopping area. An alternative is to provide a surface-level car park on the outskirts of towns. Park-and-Ride schemes encourage drivers to leave their cars outside the town, and yet have access right into the town centre (fig. 9.13). This stops the worry of not being able to find a place to park or having to pay high parking fees in the centre.

Why can a car park be at surface-level on the outskirts yet has to be multi-storey near a town centre?
Not allowing car traffic into the centre of a town can be a disadvantage to some people. Who might these be?

Fig. 9.15. With space, flowers, trees and seats, an attractive environment has been designed in the very heart of Plymouth, a city with a population of nearly ¼ million.

The Quedam Centre in Yeovil became a pedestrian precinct in 1985. A survey was made of how its 300 hectares and 10,000 m² of floor space was being used in 1987. It was found that some of the space was occupied by large departmental stores – e.g. plots 30, 46 and 49 in fig. 9.16. People often feel, rightly or wrongly, that they receive the benefit of more personal attention when shops and other services are small. An attempt has been made to provide this, for example in plots 4 to 13. But do we have a conflict here? Town centre sites are valuable. They are expensive to buy or rent. If plots are small, they may not attract enough customers to pay for these high costs and traders often find it difficult to make ends meet. So the ownership of these plots is often changing. Perhaps this was the reason why, at the time of the survey, five plots in the Quedam Centre were 'vacant' or 'to let'.

Fig. 9.16. The base-map used in the study of the 49 plots of land in the Quedam Centre, Yeovil.

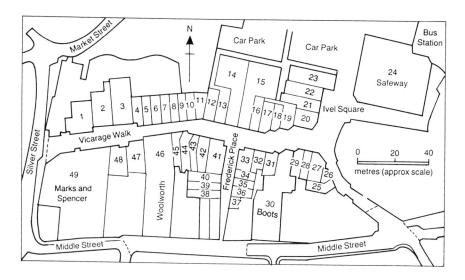

Plot 24 is a food supermarket. What advantages does it have in being sited next to (a) a large public car-park, and (b) the town's bus station? Now write down any disadvantages which this site could have.

Moving town functions outside

In this chapter, we have identified certain reasons why it has become more and more difficult to provide and use shops and other services which are sited in the centre of a town.

Make a list of as many of these reasons as you can.

One way of overcoming these difficulties is to build a **Hypermarket** (or Superstore) in the rural area just outside a town. Here, in large one-storey buildings, a household can obtain a wide range of goods and services under one roof – groceries, banking, cafeteria, garden goods, travel services, etc. A very large car park and petrol services are also provided. A random sample (see page 18) of 50 people leaving the Gateway Superstore on the northern edge of Bristol (fig. 9.17) were interviewed one Thursday morning. A schedule was completed for each person by asking the following questions and recording the answers in the table.

(a) From which town or village have you come today?
(b) How have you travelled here today?
(c) How often do you usually come here?
(d) Why do you shop here?

(a) Home town or village					
(b) Transport	walk	car	bus	bike	other
(c) Frequency of visit	more than once a week	once a week	once a fortnight	once a month	less than once a month
(d) Reasons for shopping here	pleasant surroundings	cheaper goods	wider choice	better parking	easier to buy bulky goods

Table 34 *The answers to questions (a) and (c) have been combined and are shown in a matrix.*

		How often usually visit					
		more than once a week	once a week	once every two weeks	once a month	less than once a month	Total
Distance travelled (km)	less than 10	6	7	2	4	2	21
	11–30		7	4	1	0	12
	31–50		1	2	3	3	9
	51–70			2	1		3
	over 70				5		5
	Total	6	15	10	14	8	50

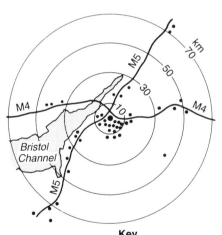

Key
● Gateway Superstore
· Shopper's Home

Fig. 9.17. The location of the Gateway Superstore, and the approximate home locations of those who answered question (a) that Thursday morning during half-term in October 1987.

matrix
A table of information which shows the links between different parts of the data (see also fig. 7.14).

Describe the pattern of location of the homes of those interviewed. Why might so few of them come from areas to the south east and north west of the Superstore? Put into your own words the data shown in Table 34.

10 Looking ahead

In previous chapters we have identified many changes within the region which are likely to continue into the future. These have included:

in Chapter 2 (a) a population increasing in number mainly as a result of people moving into it;

(b) a strain being put upon existing services as the population becomes more elderly;

in Chapter 4 (a) more demand for resources (like water) as the population and its standard of living increase;

(b) increasing awareness of how changes can lead to a conflict of interests;

in Chapter 5 (a) more farm land being used for activities other than producing food;

(b) reducing the harmful effects which farming can have on the environment and its wildlife;

in Chapter 6 (a) a growth of high-tech. industries requiring a highly-skilled labour force;

(b) large increases in the numbers of people employed in the service occupations.

For each of the chapters 7, 8 and 9, write down two changes now taking place in the South West which the text suggests are likely to continue.

'Massive change in next decade'

THE shape and nature of Britain's agricultural industry will have to undergo a massive change during the next decade, with up to four million hectares of UK land being taken out of food production by the end of the century.

That was the message from a former president of the Country Landowners' Association, Mr John Quicke, speaking in Exeter.

Mr Quicke, a member of the Devon CLA's branch committee and a countryside commissioner, chaired the Countryside Commissions Policy Review panel whose recommen-dations on maintaining the country-side and the rural economies were published recently.

Mr Quicke told Devon landowners that caring for the countryside was likely to become an increasing source of rural income and employment.

Planning

Farmers and landowners had to learn to diversify, to generate non-agricultural income — but that also meant a new approach from planners as well.

"The guidelines and the priorities of planning in rural areas will have to be changed. We have had one system of planning now for 40 years and, like in farming, the time has perhaps come for a change," he said.

Ways of making income from increased access and recreation were not obvious, otherwise every farmer and landowner would be doing it already, but Mr Quicke said that with the need for a change of direction in agriculture, farmers had to look positively at what resources were available to them.

"The emphasis has to be shifted from food production to other forms of income for the landowner," he said.

Fig. 10.1. A view of future 'massive change' as seen by a leading member of the Country Landowners' Association.

Having read fig. 10.1,
(a) what effects could a large decrease in the amount of land being used for food production have upon the South West's population and employment?
(b) suggest what alternative forms of income could be developed for a South West landowner;
(c) speculate on the impact which such changes could have upon the environment of the South West.

Fig. 10.2. A simplified map taken from the Devon County Structure Plan. It shows the location of the proposed main areas of change and the areas of high quality environment.

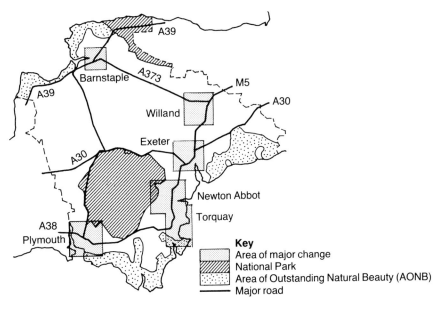

Key
Area of major change
National Park
Area of Outstanding Natural Beauty (AONB)
Major road

Planning the future

Each of the seven counties of South West England has to plan for those changes which are likely to occur within its boundaries. This is done by means of a **County Structure Plan**. The current Plan for Devon, for example, examines the expected increase in the county's population up to the year 1996. It then considers the issues which are likely to result from this. The Plan:

(a) calculates that 66,000 new dwellings will be needed;
(b) locates five main areas where this building should be concentrated (fig. 10.2);
(c) identifies the space needed for another 68,000 jobs;
(d) plans for 93,000 square metres of new shopping floor-space;
(e) proposes 57 schemes for new major roads;
(f) encourages the development of more caravan and camping sites;
(g) supports the building of minor roads to help rural areas, and specifies new routes for heavy goods traffic.

All these competing claims for space and finance are weighed up against each other while keeping in mind the need to
(i) protect historic sites and buildings of special interest;
(ii) conserve areas of high quality environment (fig. 10.2).
The County Plan is a framework into which all the decisions and more detailed planning at **District** and local levels have to fit. Sometimes the expected changes in population do not occur. Then major alterations have to be made to the County Structure Plan.

Each **District** (see page 11) is sub-divided into local town or parish council areas. Councillors are elected to look after the interests of these areas.

alternative energy

New sources of energy, especially renewable ones (see page 79) which have not been used in the past; or existing energy sources being developed in new ways.

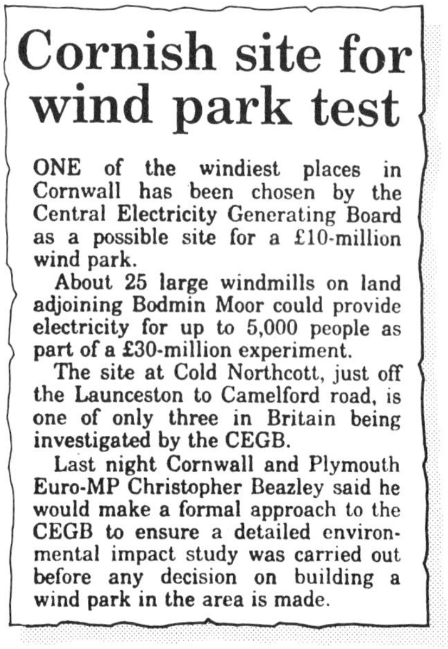

Cornish site for wind park test

ONE of the windiest places in Cornwall has been chosen by the Central Electricity Generating Board as a possible site for a £10-million wind park.

About 25 large windmills on land adjoining Bodmin Moor could provide electricity for up to 5,000 people as part of a £30-million experiment.

The site at Cold Northcott, just off the Launceston to Camelford road, is one of only three in Britain being investigated by the CEGB.

Last night Cornwall and Plymouth Euro-MP Christopher Beazley said he would make a formal approach to the CEGB to ensure a detailed environmental impact study was carried out before any decision on building a wind park in the area is made.

Fig. 10.4. Cornwall has been chosen as one of only three locations for investigations into the use of wind power. The site is shown in fig. 10.5.

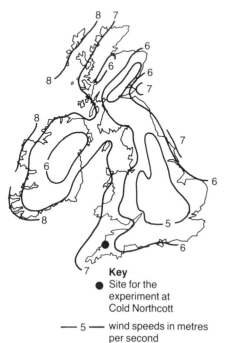

Key
● Site for the experiment at Cold Northcott

—— 5 —— wind speeds in metres per second

Fig. 10.5. Annual average wind speeds in the British Isles. The lines are called 'isovents'.

'Alternative energy'

The South West is a region in which several investigations are taking place into using alternative types of energy.

Wind has been a useful source of energy in the past. For centuries, windmills have been used widely for many purposes, including grinding corn and pumping water. But for any future large-scale use, this traditional and picturesque form of technology has to be altered a good deal. To be effective, a modern version – a wind turbine, or aerogenerator – has to be very large, about 50 m high with helicopter-like blades 70 m in diameter (fig. 10.3). As a result it could be regarded as an eyesore within the environment.

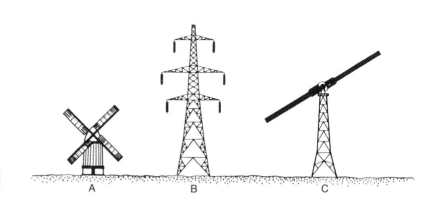

Fig. 10.3. This compares the size of an aerogenerator (C) with a traditional windmill (A) and a pylon carrying a 400 kV electric power cable (B).

An aerogenerator is cheap to run, but it can produce only 3 MW of electricity, so a large number of them is needed if wind power is to make a major contribution to power production.

Look back at Table 8. How many aerogenerators would be needed to replace the contribution now made by
(a) the three hydro-electric power stations in the South West;
(b) the Hinkley Point 'A' power station?

The central column of the aerogenerator rotates as the wind changes direction. However, like a windmill, it can only operate when the wind is strong enough to turn the blades. Fig. 10.4 locates one site in Cornwall which could be suitable. We can see from fig. 10.5 that the headlands of Land's End, the Lizard, Start Point and Hartland Point could also be suitable sites, because they are so windy. The four headlands are named on the map on page 4. Because these locations are rather remote, the cost of distributing power from them to the areas of large demand would be high. Aerogenerators are likely, therefore, to be used to meet small local demands, for example on isolated farms as a back-up to other sources of power.

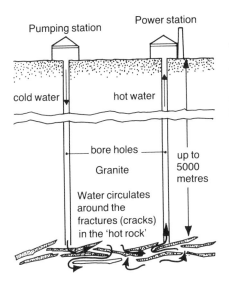

Fig. 10.6. How hot water can be obtained from the earth's interior.

'Hot rocks'

Temperatures increase as one goes deeper into the earth's crust. As long ago as Roman times, the natural heat of water beneath the city of Bath was used for enjoyment (fig. 7.15). This water has a temperature of 48 °C, too low for power generation, but research is now going on into the use of underground 'hot rocks' as a possible source of future energy. Experiments are taking place at Stithians, near Camborne, where the underlying granite (Chapter 3) offers suitable conditions. Two holes have been drilled 2,000 metres deep. Water is pumped down one of the holes. It circulates around the 'hot' granite, picking up heat, to reach a temperature of 150 °C. It is then pumped to the surface through the second hole (fig. 10.6). This super-heated water is fed into generators to produce electricity.

Power from the sea

The flow of the tide is another source of alternative and renewable energy. One of the best sites for this is the Severn estuary, because it has the particularly high **tidal range** of 30 metres. The possibility of building a large barrage across this estuary to harness the energy of the tides has been discussed since 1925. However, as other sources of electricity have become more and more costly, and as some of these sources are **non-renewable**, further investigations have been undertaken recently to see how economic such a scheme really is.

A 16 km long barrage between Lavernock Point and Brean Down is one suggested location (fig. 10.7). The islands of Flat Holm and Steep Holm could then be used as part of the structure of the barrage. As it flowed in, the tide would form a lake behind the barrage. When it flowed out, twice a day, the water would turn generators for 5 to 6 hours to produce 6,000 kW of electricity. The times of tides, however, change throughout the year and power would only be available at these times.

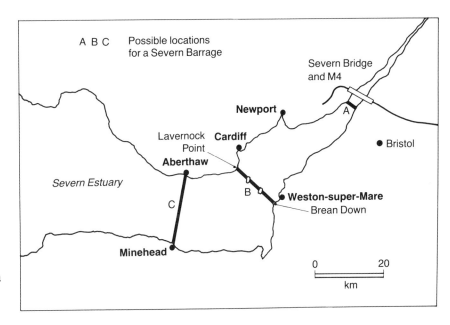

Fig. 10.7. Three possible locations for a barrage across the estuary of the River Severn.

Referring to Chapter 8 and Table 8, assess how useful supplies of electricity produced from tidal power might be in meeting demands through the national grid system of the CEGB.

Locks would allow shipping to continue using the docks located in the upper parts of the estuary. Fish would also be able to move up and down the waterway. The Department of Energy estimates that 6% of Great Britain's total electricity needs could be supplied by this barrage. It would cost £6,000 million and take ten years to build. 20,000 jobs would be created during its construction. About 500 permanent staff would be needed to operate it.

The tide already has important functions. It scours the silt which is deposited by the River Severn in the upper part of the estuary. It also flushes effluent from Severnside and **crude sewage** discharged by towns upstream. Building the barrage would have a great influence on these functions.

crude sewage
Household waste in its original state; it has not been treated to make it harmless.

For what purposes could the lake behind the barrage be used?
What damage to the environment could occur (a) during construction, and (b) after its completion?
Besides holding back water, what other use could be made of the actual structure of the barrage?

Two other possible lines for a barrage are also being studied (A and C in fig. 10.7). As the estuary widens, a barrage becomes more expensive to build. However, the tidal range increases, and so Barrage C could provide more of Britain's electricity needs.

1. If we accept the statement that 'Great Britain will require much more electricity in the future', do you think it would be better to provide this by means of a Severn Barrage or another nuclear power station at Hinkley Point? In coming to your conclusion, weigh up carefully the advantages and disadvantages of the two schemes for both the local area and the nation as a whole.
2. Argue the case for and against spending large sums of money at the present time on research into alternative sources of energy for the United Kingdom.

The year 1992 is a most important one for the European Community. Why? How might South West England be affected?

All these changes are taking place within this one region of the United Kingdom. Your attention has already been drawn to the fact that the region is situated on the periphery of Western Europe. The future of the South West and of the people living within it will also be influenced by the changes likely to take place in this larger region of the European Community.

Index

Page numbers in italics refer to tables or illustrations.